OVERLAND 1970

DAVID SHIRREFF

Published in 2022 by Crunch Books, 68 Boileau Road, London SW13 9BP

The moral right of the author has been asserted according to the
Copyright, Designs and Patents Act 1988

Copyright © 2022 David Shirreff

Cover design by Bookconsilio
www.bookconsilio.com
Front cover photograph by Andrew Craig
Back cover photographs by Hans Roodenburg hansroodenburg.nl/trail/

All rights are reserved. No part of this publication may be reproduced, stored or introduced into a retrieval system, or transmitted, in any form, or by any means (electronic, mechanical, photocopying, recording or otherwise) without prior permission in writing of the publisher and copyright holder.

A CIP record for this book is available from the British Library
ISBN: 978-0-9932969-4-9

TO JANE

ACKNOWLEDGMENTS

I am grateful to Andrew Craig and Clive Arup, two fellow travellers from the 1970s, for their photos and memories of those days. I would like to thank Valerie Potter for correcting and improving the text, and Adam Preston for his editorial guidance and for bringing the book to publication.

INTRODUCTION

Between September 1970 and September 1971, I worked for Intertrek as a driver and tour guide. Intertrek was one of the many companies set up during that era to drive paying passengers along the so-called Hippie Trail. This led from Europe – generally London – through Turkey, Iran, Afghanistan, Pakistan, India and ultimately to Nepal. Kathmandu was usually the final destination, though the more adventurous would then spend time trekking in the Himalayas.

Many people travelled the Hippie Trail independently in VW camper vans, Land Rovers, red London buses, ambulances or standard saloon cars. Or they took local buses, or hitch-hiked, bumming rides from trucks and other vehicles on the route.

Intertrek found a niche offering "expeditions" which took groups there and back and had a declared aim, such as studying Gurkha villages, or the trade route from Nepal into Tibet. But the main purpose was to avoid having to fill the vehicle for the return journey with a rag-bag of new and mostly penniless passengers picked up in Kathmandu.

So Intertrek's clients were far from being hippies themselves. They were largely middle-class, aged between eighteen and forty, in search of adventure, but not quite footloose enough to do it on their own.

The drivers, or expedition leaders as they were grandly called, were an odd bunch: some ex-military, others fresh out of university in no hurry to settle down, others hardened wanderers looking for the perfect landscape, doss-house, roadside restaurant, crystal-clear mountain pool. All of them were required to be reasonable mechanics, good drivers, diplomatic when necessary and cool-headed in a crisis. Occasionally, of course, the mask slipped. The "expedition leader" had to fight hard to win back his lost credibility.

The route was fascinating and cannot be travelled safely today. Rory MacLean, a historian and travel writer, retraced the Hippie Trail in 2001, when it briefly became doable again, and wrote an account, *Magic Bus*, of how the trail changed the travellers' lives and affected the places they travelled. Richard Gregory, who first did the Hippie Trail in 1974, still updates his website with new bits of Overland and Hippie Trail nostalgia. Both writers make the important distinction between hippies and overlanders on the Hippie Trail. The travelers' motives were somewhat different: the hippies went mainly in search of mystic and drug-induced experiences, the overlanders were driven mainly by the travel bug.

But on Intertrek journeys something else was in play, for me equally fascinating. That was the interaction of a dozen or so human beings trapped in a capsule. For three-and-a-half months they were condemned to keeping each other company, in sickness and in health, in empty desert, among the throngs of India's Grand Trunk Road, and at twelve thousand feet in the Himalayas. They were as much affected by each other as by their environment. Pairs formed and often found those liaisons hard to sustain.

Sometime in the 1970s I tried to distil my experiences

during several trips into a single fictional account. I was prompted, after meeting Rory MacLean in 2016, to look at the manuscript again. As I read it I began to wonder whether it would be of interest as a little piece of history, especially for any of those who actually did one of these trips. So here it is. No character I met then was exactly like any of the people described here, so my fellow travelers will have difficulty recognising themselves. But there are many elements of actual people and actual experiences woven into the story.

LONDON, OCTOBER 1970

ACROSS THE ROAD from the taxi rank at King's Cross Station stood an incongruous vehicle: a grey long-wheel-based Land Rover with white jerry cans clamped to its front bumper. It had a large roof-rack. A young man with long black hair stood on it, stowing canvas bags under a grey tarpaulin. Behind the Land Rover was a trailer, a metal box on wheels, to which more spare wheels and jerry cans were attached.

Eleven other people, eight men and three women aged between nineteen and forty, were standing by the wagon - awkwardly because this was the first time they had met. The women drifted towards each other seeking safety in numbers. They were conscious - or they imagined - that they were already being eyed up by one or two of the men.

Craig, the driver and expedition leader, in his late-twenties, with a weather-beaten face, explained a few points about the vehicle and its contents.

"The white jerry cans are for water, the khaki ones for petrol and the grey ones for paraffin – don't get them mixed up."

"Where do we all sit?" asked Jen, a slim woman in a loose-fitting dress.

"I'm coming to that," said Craig. All the passengers were curious about this. The Land Rover looked as though it would barely seat six people, let alone a dozen.

"The trailer contains the food and cooking materials and the tents. The tents are five-man Maréchal tents and sleep six people."

"I imagine that will be a squash," said Rudolf, a man of about forty, with a moustache.

"You'll get used to it," said Craig. "Just as you'll get used to the seating arrangements in the wagon: two up front beside the driver, three in the next row of seats, and three along each side at the back." Somebody whistled incredulously. It was Marshall, an American, also about forty.

"And where do we put our stuff?" asked Jen.

"In your kitbags, which Rick is stowing on the roof. Or in the lockers that you'll find under the rear seats." Rick was a trainee driver in his early twenties. He was struggling to cram the kitbags onto the roofrack and cover them with the grey tarpaulin, tied down with a lattice-work of rope. Thomas, an outsize teenager with enormous hands and feet, was helping him.

"Right, you'd better get in," said Craig. "We have a ferry to catch." With many grunts and efforts not to touch each other the eleven strangers settled themselves into some kind of order. Val, a solidly-built woman in her late twenties secured a place in the front next to Craig. Outsize Thomas squeezed in beside her.

"I've got long legs," he said.

"You'll all have your turn in the front," said Craig.

Quintin, a man with long side-burns, in his mid-thirties, preferred to sit in the back. He took out a book, *Diary of a Nobody*, and immediately began reading. The window-panes of the Land Rover started to fog up.

"Don't we have air-conditioning?" asked Conrad. He was an American in his early twenties.

"It'll be fine when we get going," said Marshall, a fellow American. "The General has it all worked out."

"The General?"

"Craig of course. Our expedition leader."

"Do I detect a note of sarcasm?" asked the moustachioed Rudolf.

"Not at all!" said Marshall, smiling. "These guys are highly trained, competent people. Aren't you, Rick?"

"Well, I'm on a steep learning curve. But Craig is a seasoned driver. He's done this route thousands of times."

"That's statistically impossible," said Marshall.

"Anyway. He has bags of experience."

The Land Rover left King's Cross and headed south through the London suburbs. There was no hurry for the travellers to get acquainted with each other. They knew they were in for a long haul - around fourteen weeks, mostly in this confined space six feet by ten. If they hadn't thought about it before they were beginning to realise the implications now.

The travellers fell roughly into the following categories:

THE DRIVERS:
Craig – main driver and expedition leader, late-twenties. Craggy face and gives the impression he has seen it all before.
Rick – Craig's trainee assistant, early twenties, tall, long-haired, handsome and gentle

PRE-UNIVERSITY (LATE TEENS):
Simon – small, blond and pretty, educated at Winchester, destined for medical school.

Steve – tall, black curly hair, northerner, with a chip on his shoulder
Thomas – large-limbed, clumsy, budding intellectual, destined for Cambridge

THE THIRTYSOMETHINGS:
Quintin – mid-thirties, gay, thoughtful, well-read
Rudolf – late thirties, balding, with Edwardian moustache and manner

THE WOMEN:
Gwyneth (Win) – early twenties, compact, Welsh,
Jennifer (Jen) – early twenties, posh accent, slim, beautiful,
Valerie (Val) – late twenties, well-built, easy-going,

THE AMERICANS:
Marshall – late thirties, pedantic, creature of habit
Conrad – mid-twenties, small, laid-back

DOVER, ENGLAND

IN THE HOLD of the cross-channel ferry the grey Land Rover and its trailer looked small, squeezed between giant trucks. The passengers, eager to escape the reek of diesel, made their way in twos and threes to the ship's canteen.

"Let me buy you a drink," said Jen to Craig.

"Tea."

"She's sucking up to him already," said Thomas. "I've heard about drivers' perks."

"What do you mean?" asked Simon innocently. Blond, pretty, he was the smallest and youngest of the group and had already caught the attention of Quintin who was twice his age. Thomas, big, awkward, and the next youngest, announced proudly that he was going to Cambridge next year.

"To read what?" asked Steve, the northerner.

"Philosophy."

"That won't do you much good on this trip." Steve, not much older, with a mass of dark, curly hair, was setting himself up as the people's tribune. "You're both public school, aren't you?"

"Who?" asked Thomas.

"You and Simon."

"So what?"

"Born with silver spoons in your mouth."

"My parents made great sacrifices to send me to Haileybury. I suspect yours had other priorities."

"Like going down the pub?" Steve turned back to his sausage and chips.

When they reached Zeebrugge, the passengers were asked to return to their cars. Steve was late. The ferry doors had opened and the trucks were beginning to roll out.

"We should leave without him," said Marshall, the senior American. "The Greyhound bus waits for no man." But Steve finally appeared.

"What the hell were you doing?" asked Craig.

"Nothing."

They drove through Belgium and joined the German Autobahn system. From the motorway as they crossed the Rhine they saw the black twin spires of Cologne cathedral. There was hardly any chance to take in the landscape as they chugged down the motorway at no more than fifty-five miles an hour. Conversation was difficult while they were on the road, because of the noise. It was only at service stations that they had the opportunity to learn a little more about each other. Marshall and Conrad, the two Americans, were naturally drawn to each other's company – Marshall the leader, Conrad the led. The three youngsters, blond Simon, big Thomas and northern Steve, were circling each other like cats. Two of the women, posh Jen and well-endowed Val, had already formed an alliance – disappearing to the rest-rooms together. Win, the little Welsh woman, kept more to herself.

Edwardian Rudolf closely monitored the route that Craig was taking.

"I was hoping we could visit Nuremberg," he said, "scene of thos Nazi rallies and the trials that condemned the ringleaders."

"No time, I'm afraid," said Craig. "We have to get to Istanbul inside a week."

Somewhere in Bavaria, before it got dark, Craig found a lakeside campsite.

"It has good washrooms," he said.

He showed them how to pitch the tents. These were ridge tents with an inner shell of light cotton attached to a groundsheet and hung from a cross-bar between two aluminium poles. A heavier fly-sheet was thrown over the cross-bar and pegged tight.

"They used tents like these for the last Everest expedition," said Craig.

"You mean Mallory and Irving?" asked Rudolf, twirling his moustache.

"Nothing to it," said Craig as Thomas and the three women struggled with the flysheet. He left them to put up the second tent.

"This is an initiative test," said Thomas.

"Which I'm determined to fail," said Steve.

Craig also taught them how to light the paraffin stove, using a spoonful of methylated spirit to pre-heat the burner. The little group spent their first night under canvas, crammed head to toe in the two tents. Craig was not among them.

"I bet he's gone to a hotel," said Steve. But in the morning they found Craig stretched out in his sleeping bag under the sky.

"What happens if it rains?" asked Jen.

"It seldom does."

Later that morning they spent two hours in Salzburg, sightseeing and shopping for food, before heading for eastern Austria and Central Europe. First, Yugoslavia, a string of disparate countries linked by the Autoput, a two-lane highway over one thousand kilometres long - one of the most dangerous in the world. At intervals along its verge lay the remains of smashed vehicles, a grim reminder of the Autoput's hypnotic powers. It was the main route for Turkish workers shuttling between Germany and Anatolia, racing to get home often without stopping overnight.

"How can people crash on a perfectly straight road?" asked Thomas.

"Well, there's the evidence," said Craig. "Every one of those wreaths tells a tale."

They survived the Autoput, left Communist-but-Westernised Yugoslavia and entered Bulgaria.

"This is the real thing," said Marshall. "We're now behind the Iron Curtain." There was a sense that Marshall, the American, knew what he was talking about. Rudolf had started a rumour that "the US Marshall" was with the CIA.

When they reached the capital, Sofia, instead of looking for a campsite they stopped at the entrance of a luxury hotel.

"We can't afford to stay here, can we?" said Jen, who seemed to have more money than most.

"Yes we can," said Craig. At the prevailing exchange rate the room tariff was two US dollars a night. For another two dollars they ate prime steak in the plush dining-room while a small band played and a handful of well-dressed couples danced formally.

Thomas later wrote in his diary:

We've really landed on our feet. Here we are a motley, ill-dressed crew, driving through Communist Bulgaria, suddenly pitched into the higher echelons of society. We can stay at the finest hotel, eat high off the hog, and feast our eyes on the jeunesse dorée *of*

Sofia on their dance-floor. It's a strange experience – like the clash of two cultures. I have more buying-power, but I definitely feel inferior.

Val, looking for action, persuaded Rick, the handsome trainee driver, to get up and dance. She had a strong, well-covered body which could move enticingly. She danced close to Rick with none of the formal distance observed by the Bulgarians in their suits and frocks. And she had the effect she wanted, which was to make Craig take notice. When she had finished with Rick and turned to Craig, he followed her obligingly onto the dance floor. She pressed her body close to his and felt him stirring. "Mission accomplished," she told herself.

Quintin watched the pair, reflecting that he could never dance so closely with a man – not in public, not in a month of Sundays. Then it occurred to him that a month of Sundays was not very long. "Stupid expression," he muttered.

"Stupid what?" asked Rudolf, raising an eyebrow.

In light rain the next morning they drove through the empty, almost carless, streets of Sofia to the main square. On one grandiose building festooned with hammer-and-sickle banners was a large red panel bearing the portraits of three men: Todor Zivkov, the country's leader since 1954, Vladimir Ilyich Lenin with his goatee, and Friedrich Engels with a full beard.

"I wouldn't like to tussle with those guys," said Marshall.

"You won't have to," said Craig, "two out of the three are dead."

By midday they reached the Turkish border and there was a sudden lifting of spirits. This was a colourful, half-Westernised country. After the impenetrable Cyrillic street signs in Bulgaria they could read the Turkish lettering on shops and advertisements: "Lokanta, Oto, Bira, Marshall Boya."

"That's my paint factory," said Marshall.

At the border city of Edirne they saw the grand Selimiye mosque with its four minarets reaching like pencils into the sky. By evening they were on the outskirts of Istanbul at a seaside camping-site.

FLORYA, NEAR ISTANBUL, TURKEY

It was possible to see in the lamplight the jerks of a pair of lovers. Light fell on the moving buttocks of the man. The woman's pale thigh changed shape against the sand. In harmony with the surprised breaths of the woman the man moaned. Ten metres away, a gentle orchestration was provided by the sea. Quintin sipped his lager on the veranda. Through the oleander bushes, it was possible to see the lovers. He listened to their music above the music of the bar. He analysed the sounds and saw two desperate souls, naked before God. They were trying to hide inside each other. Pathetic. Disgusting. He sipped his beer.

Lights blazed across the Sea of Marmara. A few Turks danced to the music at the bar. An aeroplane screamed out from the airport and hung its lamps over the water.

When Quintin had recovered from the noise, Rick was beside him. The long-haired youth poured his Tuborg into a glass and sat down.

"You seem very pre-occupied," said Rick.

"I have just been observing life in the raw," said Quintin and continued to look towards the islands.

"Oh? If you ask me, this place is pretty cushy."

Quintin smiled. "It's the creature man who is so desolate. Trying to burrow in wherever he can. Look down there. Do you see your honourable mentor?"

Rick peered into the bushes. He saw the bare back of the woman framed by the shoulders of the man. They were sitting up.

"Is that Craig?" Admiration and envy swept in turn over his face. The two men looked at the man and the woman. The woman took up her bra, fastened it, and twisted the cups onto her breasts. She let herself be kissed by the man and bent her head back. She stood up, pulled on her knickers and stepped into her skirt. The man sat cross-legged and naked, studying her. She took her blouse, flicked her hips twice at the man and pulled it on over her head. She waited for the man to put on his shirt and trousers. Then they walked to the edge of the sea.

"I wonder how long that will last," said Rick. "She was all over him at the restaurant. You could see what was going to happen."

"I noticed about three days ago." Quintin sipped his beer. "Last night in Sofia she made her play for him. So the lion gets his share. Are you disappointed?" He smiled at Rick.

"No, but I find her quite sexy. Craig's the boss, though, isn't he. He gets all the perks. You can see how they fall for his tough, irritated manner." He drank. "People accuse me of being effeminate. He'd never be accused of being effeminate."

"On the other hand, I find you very beautiful, but I don't suppose that turns you on one bit." Rick looked at Quintin in an amused way.

"For a moment I thought you were being completely serious." Quintin smiled to himself. He looked at the headlights of a plane as it sank over their heads.

"We're only a week out," he said, "and already I feel that this trip is mainly about us. We'll learn a lot about each other."

"Craig says you learn disgustingly little."

"I think that may be more a reflection of Craig than anything else."

"Ah. Do you see chinks in his armour? I thought everyone worshipped him."

"You shouldn't say things like that. You should come leaping to his defence. Isn't he supposed to be forming you in his own image? I'm sure he's got all the qualities you need for the job."

"Such as?"

"Arrogance, self-confidence, aggression, lust, scorn of feeble old queens like me."

"Nonsense. I'm sure he has a sneaking respect for everyone. We're all different."

"Very sneaking in my case."

"But he's your hired servant. He's paid to look after you. If you're not getting the best use out of him you must pull rank."

"I have no wish to pull rank. I admire him. He's not a servant, he's a lion. Look at him. A magnificent beast in superb condition. A bit shagged out perhaps, but that's to be expected."

"So you're happy that the trip appears to be run for his benefit."

"Why not? I dread to think what it would be like if it were run for my benefit, or Marshall's. God forbid."

"Marshall strikes me as being slightly mad."

"British understatement."

"He seems to think we won't get anywhere unless he personally sees to it. Gold-rimmed spectacles, binoculars, vitamin tablets, the lot. Remarkable mind though, you must admit. He reads Chinese and says he's a ballistics expert. Makes you wonder what he's doing on a tour like this. Rudolf says he's a lackey of the CIA."

"Talk of the devil. There he is with Rudolf." The veranda was a large one, dotted with chairs and tables, except for a dancing area in the centre. The Turks twisted about to Western music. Marshall and Rudolf map in hand wove their way through the dancers to an empty table which looked clean. Marshall picked up a single lemonade bottle, emptied it and put it on another table.

"Making sure they're not bugged," whispered Quintin. "I wonder what conspiracy is being hatched now."

"But Rudolf – I call him 'Edwardian Rudolf' - can't be an American agent. He's a British upper-class twit!"

"Ahah! You too have failed to penetrate his devilish disguise."

Edwardian Rudolf unfolded the map and spread it over the table. His chinless face with its week's growth of beard began to bob up and down. References and scales were studied. His hair was short, revealing a bald patch at the crown. His thin body was lost in a large roll-neck sweater. "By my reckoning we should take four days to get through Turkey."

"Which route is that?" Marshall craned his head close to Rudolf's shoulder, then twisted it so that he could see the map the right way up.

"Straight as a die through the middle." Marshall bent even closer to the paper. His gold-rimmed spectacles played tricks at such an angle. Rudolf found himself looking into the hood of Marshall's anorak.

"Charming sight," he muttered to himself.

"I would say four days, mebbe even five days. What does the General say?"

"He wouldn't know. He says time is immaterial. 'Time, Rudolf,' he told me, 'is a figment of the imagination, it doesn't exist'."

"When was that?"

"About twenty minutes ago. As he was disappearing somewhere with that Val woman. I thought we were supposed to be having a meeting tonight."

Marshall looked up at the dancing Turks. There was no expression on their faces. They were fashionably dressed and their bodies moved self-consciously.

"Perhaps we could call our own meeting," he said. A waiter collected lemonade and beer bottles from the neighbouring tables. Marshall followed his movements with his eyes narrowed. "Then we can tell him what we want to do."

"I think it's about time some responsibility was shown in running this trip, I must say," said Rudolf. "Half the people haven't got the wit to know what's happening to them. They must be informed. We must see that the journey follows what was laid down in the brochure."

"I think we can do better than the brochure. The brochure is a kind of base level. We should be able to go further and see more than is stipulated in the brochure. Craig's gotten used to his own pace. If we get tough we can get the best out of him. Should he for instance be allowed to fraternise with a woman?"

"I say, I don't think we can stop that sort of thing."

"But there's no doubt that it weakens a man, physically, and it saps him of his will-power."

"It makes him easier to live with." Marshall looked long and hard at Rudolf. If they were to achieve anything they must not disagree.

"What about his henchman?" he said. "Can't we get some more sense out of him? He's on the company payroll, isn't he?"

"Rick's a nice lad. Or should we say he hasn't been corrupted yet."

"Well, we must get him on our side before he does get corrupted. He's over there with Quintin."

"Odd fish, Quintin. You get the impression nothing would

upset him. But perhaps that sort of person is the first to go to pieces."

"We'll see, won't we." Marshall pressed his hands on the table and stood up. For a moment he stayed in this forward position, shoulders hunched, as if making sure of his objective. Then he launched himself in the direction of Rick and Quintin. Rudolf watched him, hands clasped on the table.

"Don't look now," said Quintin, "but here comes our friend from the CIA." Rick involuntarily turned round.

"Howdy Marshall," he said. "Pull up a chair." Marshall remained standing.

"Thank you. I wondered if you gentlemen would care to come over and join us. There are one or two points about the route we would like to discuss." (Marshall pronounced 'route' like 'rout')

"I had no idea we were planning a massacre," said Quintin, almost to himself.

"OK," Rick sprang up. "I haven't got much idea myself, but we can have a go, can't we."

"I'll join you later." Quintin took out a cigarette. He watched the form, almost female, of Rick's hair and shoulders beside the close-cropped head of Marshall as they returned to Rudolf. The two lovers were some way along the beach, their outlines lost in the dull foam. There was an inch of beer left in Quintin's bottle. There were three cigarette ends in the ash-tray. He wondered whether he was smoking too much. Only Win and he smoked. Strange chubby girl, her make-up beginning to smudge; femininity was splitting at the seams. She should have short hair if she can't look after it, he thought. Rick knew how to look after his hair.

Quintin brushed a curly lock behind his ear and tugged at one of his luxuriant side-burns. He brushed ash from his trousers. Clouds in the sky were spreading the moon sideways.

"God, not another one." Red and green pinpoints of light hung in the sky. Two headlights snapped on, and the beast, heavier than air, sat on its tail as it plunged downward. Behind it came the roar and whine of the turbines. "Does this go on all night, do you think?" Quintin screwed up his face and addressed the question to Win, the little Welsh girl, and her escorts "Northern" Steve and Conrad, the other American, who had just arrived to join the meeting. "Have a cigarette." He pushed the packet over to Win. They sat down with a scrunching of chairs.

"Can't be worse than the railway at home," said Steve. He slouched back in his chair. One of his legs fidgeted, apparently out of control..

"There's a railway here as well," said Quintin.

"How much does the beer cost then?"

"Four lira, unless you argue. Then it's three."

"Right!" Steve smacked his open palm onto the table. "Conrad, me old friend, will you buy us a beer?"

"Oh, is it my turn? Sure." Conrad, quiet and stocky, anxious to please, ambled to the bar. He passed Rudolf and Marshall who appeared to be in earnest consultation with Rick. On his way back Marshall touched his arm.

"Hey, could you tell the others we're having a meeting? Right over here to discuss the route."

"Sure."

Two tables were put together. Edwardian Rudolf was in the chair. The six others ranged themselves around the bottles.

"Seven of us," said Rudolf. "Where are the other five?"

"Jen, Si and Thomas went to see some Turkish dancing, I think," said Win.

"And the other two are," said Rudolf nodding seawards, "accounted for."

"Our great leader!" toasted Steve. "Here's health and long life to him!" Rick raised his glass, but no-one else did.

"More power to his elbow," he muttered. Rudolf smoothed the map in front of him.

"Now as far as I can see," he said, "from Craig's very vague hints, he intends to take us via the Black Sea. I submit that this is a waste of time. It's a hundred miles longer than the direct route and, as I understand it, we've come on this trip to get to the Himalayas, not to spend valuable time footling about Turkey. As far as I'm concerned I don't mind a bit. I'm older than most of you and I've seen a bit of the world. But for some of you this is the chance of a life-time, and you should be concerned that you get the best value out of it. Routes should be decided by you and I'm sure my good friend Rick, who has one foot in the enemy's camp, as it were, agrees with me." Rick did not look happy, but he smiled.

"We must remember," said Rick, "that Craig's a lot more experienced than we are. He knows all the ropes. I don't know about Turkey any more than you do. I'm sure it's possible to benefit from his knowledge without bearing a personal grudge as some of you seem to be doing. I like Craig and I respect him."

"My dear fellow, it's not a question of whether we like the man. I'm sure we can all see some good in him. But as you see an expedition has to be run, decisions have to be made. And if a leader loses credibility, others must take the matter out of his hands."

"Who says he's lost credibility?"

"I think we should have a committee, at any rate, to decide on the route. If his lordship condescends to give us the benefit of his vast knowledge, so much the better. But experience has shown that it isn't to be counted on." Steve stood up and clapped:

"Bravo! I'm all for a bit of righteous indignation. Bravo!"

Conrad laughed nervously and Steve sat down. He had stopped everything. "Continue," he said.

"Thank you," said Rudolf. "I'm not interested in insulting or being insulted. But I am keen to restore some common sense into this trip. Has anyone else got anything to say?" There was silence. Quintin drew on his cigarette. Marshall started to speak.

But Rick had already said "Excuse me," and left the meeting. He wove through the dancers and took the steps down to the beach. He had to find Craig. The sand made it impossible for him to walk fast but he saw the two lovers sitting on a rowing boat. As he approached he was slightly out of breath.

"Hi, Craig," he called softly and came very close to the pair of them. He leaned on the boat. "Hi," he repeated.

"Fantastic evening," said Craig. "The Marmara Sea is asleep."

"They're having a meeting," said Rick.

"Oh, what about?"

"The route." He hesitated. "And you as well. There's a feeling that you're not being very communicative."

"Ah."

"But the route's the main thing. If you can explain to them why it's better to go via the Black Sea everything will be cleared up. They're panicking a bit, that's all."

"Good. Why don't you trot along and explain it to them then?"

"But I don't know enough about the roads or anything."

"Common sense."

"But you've been there before. You know all the ropes." Craig smiled and put his hand on Rick's shoulder.

"Good luck, lad. Sweat it out, sweat it out." He turned to kiss Val who had been waiting patiently. Rick stood for a moment, undecided. Then he turned and walked against the heavy sand.

The expedition moved on the next morning. They took a ferry across the Bosphorus into Asia. Nothing had been resolved by the meeting. Craig was driving. Val sat next to him, with Rudolf on her left. The two Americans and Win, the Welsh woman, sat in the row of seats behind. In the rear of the wagon the three university candidates Thomas, Simon and Steve sat on one side, facing Rick, Jen and Quintin, who was reading *The Mill on The Floss*.

GEREDE, TURKEY

At the top of a mountain pass, they stopped at a tea shack – its window frames painted blue. Highway machines loomed large in the shade of a giant hangar.

In the tea-house Craig and Val sat apart from the others. Craig stirred sugar into his glass of tea, while Val gave him a running commentary on their relationship so far:

"I didn't think much of you at all the first time I saw you. If you must know it was Quintin I fancied first. In fact I was so impressed I thought he was leading the expedition. Not the haggard specimen who looked as though he'd just spent a night gambling – and lost!"

"You can't expect every man you have a brush with to look like a movie star."

"But you do, Craig. You look like Clint Eastwood – a bit. I think you're fantastic."

"More fool you."

"From that moment," continued Val, "I wanted you to be the one. Only you, with your mean, cruel mouth."

"You've been watching too much television."

"Haha! And where did you get that po-faced air of studied

boredom from? People don't hunch their shoulders like that in real life. Not over cups of tea. What are you afraid of, Craig?"

"Me? Why should I be afraid of anything?"

"Because you don't do just the normal things."

"Like what?"

"I mean little things like pecking me lightly on the cheek, or even smiling occasionally."

"I don't do stuff like that."

"Well, you ought to learn." Val adjusted a strand of hair on his forehead. "Go on, why don't you say it?" she continued.

"What?"

"You thought I was different, but now you find I'm like all the others."

Craig rocked onto his feet. He fumbled in his pocket and took out a handful of coins.

"Let me pay," said Val unsnapping her purse.

"What, fifty kurus? You must be joking."

"Thank you kind sir." Craig turned to the other travellers who were drinking their tea at a respectful distance. At least one of them had seen him get up. He walked out into the fresh mountain air. Green woods cascaded into deep valleys. The sky was grey. Back the way they had come heavy lorries ground up the hill. A snub-nosed BMC truck reached the flat of the pass and went by, farting characteristically through its vacuum brakes.

Steve was filling some jerry cans with water: the job for which he had volunteered. He straightened up to watch the lorry go past and waved to the grinning driver who shouted:

"Hallo Mister!"

The vacuum brakes farted again. "Disgusting," said Steve. He bent to his task again. He put a few grains of chlorine from a bottle into each can. He heaved the cans into their holders on the front bumper and snapped the padlocks shut.

"Hullo chief," he said to Craig. "Where do you think we'll get to tonight then?"

"Off this main road anyway. We'll soon be on the dirt."

"Is that corrugated road and that?"

"Some of it."

"God how tough! Do we rope together?"

"No, we just keep our mouths shut, so the dust doesn't get in."

The other members of the expedition emerged from the teahouse. They arranged themselves in the eleven seats among a nest of anoraks and books. American Conrad was squeezed into the worst seat, in the middle of the second row.

"I don't mind," he pleaded. "I've got short legs."

"Where's Vibrant Val?"

"Powdering her nose."

"Why's she called Vibrant Val?"

"Something she has in her luggage."

They waited three minutes until Val came; then they drove on.

AMASYA, TURKEY

Extract from Thomas's diary:

This is our second night in Asia. We have spent the whole day on dirt roads driving through rolling hills of farming country. Every village is the same: a mosque with its minaret, uneven streets bordered by dingy shops that are little more than holes in the wall. Tractors, Ford Transits full of stocky little men with moustaches, women dressed in veils, and livestock. The children are dressed in black and white for school. They run after the Land Rover shouting, waving with one hand and slinging a stone with the other. It is Ramadan, which means that for most of the day it's impossible to get food, even chai (tea). Turkish is a fascinating language. The one word that everyone has learnt is "Yok!" which means "no, there isn't", "we haven't any" or "get away from here", accompanied by throwing up the head and spreading out both palms like webbed feet.

We are camped about a mile from a village. It's marvellous how the Land Rover can just leave the road and take to the open country. Welsh Win and Pretty-Boy" Simon are cooking supper.

US Marshall seems to be giving them advice. He's quite interesting but a complete nut. There's nothing he won't voice an opinion on, from politics to trout tickling. Quintin in my opinion is the only really educated person on this trip. He's reading Middlemarch. *We had a conversation today about the Marowitz* Hamlet. *It's nice to find someone else who's sensitive to literature, right out here! The Turks are gathering. Two of them at the moment. They are keeping their distance, but Rudolf has got himself into conversation with one of them. Soon they will move in. Why don't they have any sense that they are intruding? The Craig/Val affair is at an interesting stage. He is obviously bored stiff of her. Probably has so many women he doesn't know what to do with them. Jen, in my opinion, is more attractive than V, although a bit horsey. The girl I can't understand is Win. She doesn't look after herself – she SMELLS! I thought Steve was going to have a go at her, but he's probably been put off for life. Rudolf has got over his explosion yesterday. He wanted to know why we weren't sticking to the brochure and going to Ankara. He's too old for anything pioneering, he ought to catch a plane. Everyone is behind Craig really, although he likes to think he's a bastard.*

I almost forgot. Last night we were held at gunpoint for half an hour. It was dark and we were driving late. Some soldiers waved us down and got us out of the car. Then they searched everywhere. Marshall had a sheath knife on him, which was confiscated. Win started to cry. But all they wanted, as we discovered, was her cigarettes. They took her last packet and let us drive on. Craig was very calm. He says it quite often happens: you have to humour them.

Simon has a sister at Cambridge. He says I must look her up when I go up next year. It sounds as though she's part of the social set – hundreds of balls and cocktail parties. I shall be going there to work!

. . .

Thomas closed his diary and put it carefully into his kitbag. His sleeping bag, which he had spread out, was getting damp from the dew. He rolled it up again and put on his anorak. The night had become cold. "Food!" was called. A blast was given on the horn of the Land Rover. The travellers came in from the gathering dark. Some sat in the vehicle, others stood waiting to be handed a plate. Win ladled out meat. Simon administered potato and vegetable. In a restrained but eager way hands reached out to take the plates. Salt was passed round. Tomato ketchup from England was shaken onto the brew. The expeditionaries were beginning to watch each other's eating habits. Northern Steve's greed with the tomato ketchup was noticed.

"A man's gotta do what a man's gotta do," he retorted.

"Do you think we ought to give those poor Turks some food?" said Jen. "They're just standing there. I'm sure they must be starving."

"They're just curious," said Marshall. "They've probably never seen a white man before."

"They're not that dark-skinned."

"They won't eat our food anyway. It would just be a waste."

"But it's not pig is it?" asked Jen.

"They still won't touch it. Try them with some." An extra plateful was spooned out.

"Hey. There's hardly enough to go round as it is," whined Steve. But the experiment was continued. Jen, with her best smile, advanced holding the plate at arm's length.

"Would you like some dinner?" The two Turkish boys smiled and shifted their weight from foot to foot. They looked at each other. One of them threw back his head and said "Yok!" softly.

"Very good Turkish food," persisted Jen. She baaed like a

sheep. The lads laughed and baaed back. Jen approached the one who had not said "Yok!" She put the plate into his hands and retired some distance. The Turks began a conference over the food. Jen came back to the Land Rover.

"I think it's best to leave them to it."

"They'll probably have the plate as well," resumed Steve.

"We can afford it," said Jen sensitively. "If they need the plate they can have it."

"Ey sey, very condescending aren't we," said Steve [mimicking Jen's posh accent]. "If they needs our lendrovah they can jolly well hev it."

"Steve!" cautioned Win.

"Stenley end Ey shell continue on foot!" Jen looked at Steve in amazement.

"I think that's swinish," she said. "We don't say anything about *your* ghastly accent."

"Well you should do. You should respond to the fact that I'm aggressively working-class. That's what we're here for, isn't it? To stir each other up. What does the brochure say? 'A young mixed group from all walks of life.' We seem to be missing out badly down my end of the scale, that's all I can say."

"Everyone is middle-class nowadays," said Thomas.

"They're what? I'm not middle-class, I'm bleeding working-class. Me dad was any road."

"The snobbery of the artisan rears its ugly head," muttered Rudolf.

"I thought we were here to study weird peoples and exotic customs of the lands we pass through," said Rick.

"No, we're here to besiege each other," said Quintin.

"To whiff the aroma of their strange languages."

"Yok!"

"Yok!"

"Besiege?" Thomas asked Quintin. "How do you mean besiege?"

"Oh. I just threw it out. You shouldn't have been listening."

"'An easy-going disposition'," shouted Steve, "'and a sense of humour are the only other requirements'. It says nothing about foreign aid for a kick-off. You haven't studied your brochures, comrades! Can I have some more spud?" He nudged Win with a smile, and she tipped a large helping of mash onto his plate. Jen turned towards the Turkish boys. They had retreated up the hill.

"They've probably been scared away by the shouting," she said.

"On the contrary they love shouting, they love violence," Marshall postulated. "When you address a Turk, especially if you insult him, you can see his eyes light up in eagerness to hit back. They're a fantastic fighting people."

"These ones are very gentle."

"They're great lovers too, Jen-baby." Marshall's eyes grinned through his spectacles. He chewed at his meat.

"I'm sure they are, Marshall," said Jen coldly. The Turks appeared again within the circle of light. Jen walked up to them and saw the plate, half empty. They brought their hands to their chests to signal that they were full up. One of them achieved the words "thank you" in English.

"You're very welcome," said Jen. She took the plate from them and stood waiting. "Would you like some tea? Chai?" They smiled and again refused. Jen hesitated. She looked round at the group of travellers. "What can we give them?" she asked.

"You're too soft," came the reply.

"Give them some pencils, they always like pencils."

"We're fresh out of pencils." Jen looked at the Turks again. She pushed her hair back and unscrewed one earring. She unscrewed the other earring. "Go on," she said. Each of them took an earring. Jen said "goodbye" and walked back to the Land Rover. The Turks remained. Supper was finished and people began to go to bed. The Turks disappeared.

Marshall slept in a two-man tent which he had acquired in Istanbul. The others, if it was a clear night, were getting used to sleeping under the stars. Thomas, half in his sleeping bag, continued to write his diary.

Steve is a good catalyst.

He looked across at posh and beautiful Jen who was always last into bed. He saw her smooth back; she was very tall. She slept in her sleeping bag with nothing on!

SIVAS, EASTERN TURKEY

Blond Simon shaved himself in the wing mirror of the Land Rover. His bowl stood on the bonnet filled with cold water. The blade scraped noisily over five days' growth of down. It was a pretty, round face, fresh from Winchester; perhaps one or two spots were beginning to affect it. He shaved because he hoped a flash of inspiration would come to him during the ritual. But he did not solve the mystery of how he had spent so much money in Turkey. He heard the groans of people getting up.

First on the scene was Edwardian Rudolf, whose hands were white with cold. He walked up and down, proud that he was ready before everyone else.

"What about this breakfast, then?" he said. "Shall I light the stove?" He rubbed his hands together.

"I'll do it in a minute," said Simon. "I thought I'd get this chore over first."

"You don't need to shave, do you? What a waste of man-hours." Rudolf rummaged in the ammunition boxes. "Where are the matches?" Simon turned round, razor poised, and his face half-covered with soap.

SIVAS, EASTERN TURKEY

"They should be there." Rudolf rummaged again.

"There should be a special place for matches," he said. "Then none of this inefficiency would arise."

"Win's got some anyway."

"Win! Where is she?" Rudolf's head darted in all directions. "My god, she's still asleep." He did not stride over and wake her up. He thrust his hands into his pockets. Looking down at his boots he took a few paces up and down.

Simon hurried his shaving. He wiped the soap from his face with a towel. He rinsed his razor, tipped the water onto the ground by the front wheel and took his equipment back to his sleeping bag. Little Welsh Win was stirring. Simon bent down beside her as she fumbled for the matches. He whistled as he prepared to light the kerosene stove.

After breakfast Marshall dismantled his tent. Others put on their hiking boots for a morning walk. Northern Steve and stocky Conrad were already small shapes in the distance, about to join the main road. The object of the morning walks, said the brochure, was to keep fit and to break their boots in for the Himalayas. Quintin preferred to read *Middlemarch*.

The two Turks appeared again. They stood at a respectful distance. One of them held some bread and goat's cheese, which he gave to Jen.

"Kalem?" said one of them softly.

"Craig, what does kalem mean?"

"Pen."

"But I've already given them my earrings."

"Give 'em an inch.... little monkeys'll take the milk out of your tea." Jen looked at the Turks. One had sores behind the ears. The nose of the other was running. They wore shabby suits and carried sticks. The one with the cold sniffed but did not wipe his nose. She looked at their naked feet stuck in rubber galoshes. "Come on Jen, everyone's ready," called Thomas. She smiled at the Turks. "Goodbye," she said, and turned to the Land Rover. They ran after it a little way, shouting as it bounced over the field.

REFAHIYE, EASTERN TURKEY

CRAIG STOPPED the Land Rover and left the engine running. He got out and asked Win to put her foot on the accelerator a few times.

"I thought so," he said. Rick got out of the back door.

"What?" he asked.

"The fuel pump's gone."

"What does that mean?"

"It means you and I get our hands dirty. We do have a repair kit."

Craig drove on. They stopped at midday for an early lunch. Rick took the tool-kit out of the trailer.

"And we'll need the spares," said Craig. The sun shone on the grove which Craig had chosen. Water gushed from a pipe embedded in concrete. "Like Moses's rock," said Quintin.

The girls took the opportunity to wash their hair. Win washed some underwear. It was the turn of Steve and Conrad to make the lunch. They spread cheese and Marmite onto thick chunks of bread. Moustachioed Rudolf was interested in the repair work. He stood with his hands in his pockets, leaning over the warm body of the engine.

"What is it? The diaphragm?" he asked.

"Probably," said Craig, fingering the spare parts.

"Ow! This is fucking hot!" Rick complained from underneath.

Over the rise of a hill in the east another vehicle appeared. It was a Land Rover. The roof-rack was laden; white jerry cans sat on the front bumper; eager faces peered out of windows. It stopped. Behind it was an identical trailer. The driver was wearing sunglasses.

"Craig!"

"Jerry!"

"Having some trouble then?"

"No. I wasn't expecting to see you for a couple of days."

"They're pushing me. They want to get back to the flesh-pots." Jerry turned to his clients. "We might as well have lunch here, hey folks?" He stepped out of the vehicle. The other travellers got out with him. Craig's expedition looked at Jerry's expedition. They did not mingle. Jerry did not take off his sunglasses. He walked up to Craig's Land Rover and looked at the engine.

"Not bad," he said. "Fuel pump? Mine went near Patna; fucking hot it was too."

"Which way did you come back?"

"Southern route, and Persepolis, bloody fantastic."

"Yuh? I don't know if we'll have time for Persepolis."

Jerry's group were exotically dressed, though dirty. There were colourful shirts among the men. Embroidery and tassels hung from their chests. Some of them wore loose cotton trousers, originally white, now stained with sweat and dirt. There were three beards. One man had shoulder-length hair. The girls wore roughly the same. One had a long cotton skirt. Some were already busy making lunch. The two expeditions gradually fused together in conversation.

"You'll meet Bullshit Tours up ahead," continued Jerry.

"Oh. What are they in?"

"Beaten-up old Transit. They had a flat battery. We had to give them a jump-start."

"Well I'm fucked if I'm going to give them a jump-start."

"They're probably alright now. Except that there's mutiny aboard. It seems they came away without any tents. What are your lot like?"

"Alright." Rudolf had already moved away.

"Which one's your concubine? That tall one?"

"You've got to be joking, have you heard her voice?"

"Well then, you haven't got much choice have you. It must be that tough-looking specimen in culottes."

"That's right."

"When?"

"Istanbul."

"Haha!" Jerry clicked his fingers. "Cologne, can you beat that?"

"The one with the big boobs, no doubt."

"That's right, Martha." Music came from the newly arrived Land Rover. Win and Thomas were drawn to look in through the door. Win performed a little dance.

"Here Marfa! Come and meet Craig!" Martha, well-covered and shapely, walked over to meet Craig. She put an arm round Jerry.

"Jerry's told me about your trip together - fantastic," she said. Her eyes were smudged with mascara. The breasts were a prominent feature.

"Isn't she great?" Jerry slapped her behind.

"Looks a fair bit of arse to me," said Craig and turned down to Rick. Martha laughed.

"How you getting on, Rick?"

"I've nearly got it off. These bolts are right buggers." He appeared with the disconnected pump.

"Isn't he sweet," said Martha to Jerry.

"Let's have a look at it," said Craig. "We'll need a screw-driver." Rick fetched a screw-driver. Together they dismantled the pump.

Blond Simon recognised a contemporary from Winchester.

"What's it like out there?" he asked.

"It's really cool man, really cool."

"I suppose you've been living off drugs. What's your Christian name. I can only remember you as Fortescue."

"Call me Forte. Like in Kathmandu they've got this really great shit, man. You can buy it in the market. It blows your mind." He giggled and put an arm on Simon's shoulder.

"How did you find India?"

"Oh India." The Wykehamist looked into the middle distance. "India is like a heap of dung with ants crawling all over it, white ants. And hot as hell."

"But didn't you see any palaces and forts, and remnants of the British Empire? I thought bits of it were just like England."

"Perhaps it was, Simon, but now it's completely swamped by bicycles and banana skins. Those poor buggers do nothing all day. You see hundreds of them by the roadside, just existing. It makes you sick."

"But what about the culture and the music? What about the Hindu temples? They can't all have disappeared."

"Oh, it's all there man, but it doesn't live any more. An Indian would rather have a Woolworth's sweater than a throne of ivory, that's what's happened to India."

"I'll probably be staying there a bit anyway. My sister's in Bombay."

"That should be alright. Europeans still have a hell of a

cushy life. You feel like a little lord, servants bringing you bathwater and all that crap."

"I might do some VSO."

"We didn't see any of those. They probably live in mud huts with the natives. Anyway Afghanistan's a freak, man. This would interest you. I bought this pistol in a junk shop. Here, it's in the wagon."

Quintin watched Forte and Simon walk to the Land Rover. He ate an apple. He was entranced by Simon's golden hair and the curve of his rump. He considered lean Forte in his loose cotton clothes. "Old school chums," he found himself saying aloud. He laughed at himself and returned to the copy of *Middlemarch* resting on his knee. But he looked up again. He saw Forte showing Simon a pistol. They cocked it and fired it at each other in turn. Music came from the Land Rover. Forte climbed inside the vehicle and put on another tape. Quintin stared at Simon standing in a dramatic pose with the pistol. "Ah, come on!" he scolded himself, and escaped into his book.

The petrol pump was dismantled. Craig fitted the new diaphragm and worked the mechanical pump with his hand.

"Well, we can put it in again now," he said. Rick was left to refit the pump.

"That's the way to make 'em learn," said Jerry. "Aren't you going to introduce me to your bit of stuff then?"

"Mm. We don't seem to be speaking at the moment." But Val appeared carrying two plates. "I saved you and Rick some lunch."

"Thanks," said Craig. "Jerry wants to meet you." Val handed Craig his plate.

"Just a moment then." She walked on towards Rick and put his plate on the front wing. "Rick, I've brought you some lunch."

"You're an angel," said Rick. Val stayed by the bonnet.

"He's leaving you all the dirty work is he?"

"That's right. White collar worker. Still, I don't complain. It's the only way to learn. I hate standing around watching other people do things."

"I could stand around watching you do things all day," said Val. Rick turned to look at her.

"Here, steady on," he said. But she had already skipped away. Rick wiped the back of his hand across his brow, then realised that it was oily. "Shit!" he said.

"Val, this is Jerry."

"She's been flirting with your second-in-command," said Jerry.

"Oh, it's about time she showed an interest in someone else on the trip."

"Craig!"

"I was beginning to think I was God."

"Of all the stuck-up bastards!"

"It's nice to be disillusioned occasionally."

"I'd say," said Jerry. He laughed uncomfortably. "Why don't you come and share a bit of lunch with my crowd?"

"Isn't that a bit dangerous? They usually howl at losing a single mouthful."

"We'll risk it." Craig followed Jerry to the back of his trailer. Val held onto his arm.

"Pig," she said. Martha greeted them with her mouth full. She beamed at Val. They leaned against the side of the Land Rover in the sun.

"You know," said Jerry, "at this stage of the trip the thing runs itself. They tell me what to do and I get on and do it. They're a great crowd."

"I don't think we've achieved that kind of symbiosis quite yet," reflected Craig.

"I had to bleeding change their nappies for them. Now they change mine, metaphorically speaking that is."

REFAHIYE, EASTERN TURKEY

"I should hope so," said Martha.

"Well, that's the way it is," said Jerry. His group had already packed up the lunch. They were in a hurry to drive on. He climbed into the driver's seat. Martha sat beside him. "See you," he said. The tape recorder started again, and the Land Rover left, leaving a slight cloud of dust.

In the silence that followed, washing up continued. Rudolf began to scold Steve and Conrad because they were playing with soap bubbles.

"Come on, you're keeping everybody waiting. You ought to think of others as well as yourselves." Bolshie Steve stopped washing up altogether.

"OK, keep your hair on," he said to Rudolf. "There's not much of it left." Marshall addressed Craig quietly:

"That bunch said they can get through Turkey in three days. Do they have a faster vehicle?"

"No, I think they must have been, as you Americans say, putting you on."

"They didn't give me that impression." Craig considered Marshall coldly:

"No, I don't suppose they would have done." Val adjusted her make-up in the wing mirror. Rick was watching her from his position thirty yards away. Only Quintin appeared totally calm as he snapped *Middlemarch* shut and took his place in the Land Rover. They drove on.

A Ford Transit sat stranded by the roadside. One wheel had sunk into in the soft slag of the embankment. Fourteen passengers stood or walked up and down the road. The driver worked underneath the front wheels. Craig immediately saw what had happened. He stopped his Land Rover within twenty yards. One of the passengers on the road shouted:

"You English?"

"We'll need the trailer off," Craig said to Rick. He got out and went to consult the Transit driver. Thomas and the others studied the strange vehicle from their seats. It was near the edge of the twenty-foot drop. It seemed that a small push would send it tumbling down the embankment. On the flank of the vehicle at this angle they could make out the legend – BULLSHIT TOURS. Rick lowered the jockey wheel of the trailer, released the coupling and unshackled the safety chain. He turned the Land Rover round so that it was nose to nose with the Transit. He fitted the hawser from his bumper to the front spring of the other vehicle.

"Right," said Craig. "We'd better have some people steadying it with a rope." A rope was slung over the top of the Ford and volunteers took the strain. Craig got into the Land Rover, engaged the lowest four-wheel gear, and signalled to the Transit driver. Together they brought the bus out of danger. The rope and hawser were disconnected. Bullshit passengers helped to re-couple the trailer. They gave Craig a bottle of whisky and waved the Land Rover goodbye.

"They're a scruffy lot."

"What a shower." Rudolf brooded: "I hope all this time we're wasting doesn't mean we're going to miss out Persepolis."

"I don't think helping people is wasting time," said Jen.

"People like that shouldn't be allowed to leave England. The whole outfit appears to be run on a shoestring."

"They looked an interesting bunch to me," said Simon.

"A lot more enterprising than you fucking lot of bourgeois softies," said Steve.

"Some of them had already spent nearly all their money."

"Now that I regard as really enterprising – almost visionary."

"They certainly seem to be living dangerously anyway.

They say they did a complete pirouette on the Autoput in Yugoslavia."

"Well I, for one, don't want to spend my last seconds falling over a cliff, Craig, *nota bene*." Rudolf tapped the driver on the shoulder.

"I've got something lined up for you which is much more lingering and personal, don't despair." Craig refused to talk any more.

"He's planning a mass murder," said Northern Steve.

ERZURUM, EASTERN TURKEY

THOMAS WROTE IN HIS DIARY:

Erzurum, capital of the Seljuk dynasty. We entered it on an extremely cold and blustery day. There are many taxis drawn by horses. Rudolf and I were doing the shopping. We planned a spaghetti Bolognese but could not get any peppers. Surprise! Craig told us this was the last place we could buy wine, so we got two big two-litre bottles. It was disgusting. The others went to have a Turkish bath. We had one ourselves later. Rudolf looked ridiculous as he emerged with towels wrapped round his head and shoulders. With his puny beard he reminded me of one of the three kings in a school nativity play. There were two Turks on the marble slab in the middle holding hands. Poor buggers don't have much chance to get off with women. Quintin and Simon had a fight over some soap. I think Qu.. might be a bit qu.. Will have to watch him. But he's highly intelligent. Bread and honey the thing to have in Erzurum. We found Cr. and Val stuffing themselves. Then Win and Jen came in. It was dark before we met back at the

Land Rover to drive out to camp. Rudolf was furious. He ranted again about who is supposed to be running this trip, and we had a vote on going to Persepolis. Six to four in favour, but Rick and Cr. did not vote.

DOGUBAYAZIT, EASTERN TURKEY

Rick lay in his sleeping bag. His fellow travellers were stretched out in ones and twos where they had found comfortable patches of earth. To his right he felt, rather than saw, the shape of Mount Ararat, a perfect cone tipped with snow and bathed in moonlight. The flat desert seemed to unfold as far as the base of the volcano and Little Ararat, below and to the right. A few miles to his left was the ruined palace of Ishak Pasha with its single dome. Rick stretched his hand up to the unblinking stars and traced the constellations that he knew: the Great Bear, the Seven Sisters, Orion the Hunter. Sometimes it was good to be alone. He drifted into sleep. A few hours later he was woken by a gentle rasping sound. It was very close to him, and getting closer. Suddenly he saw the dinosaur-like head of a tortoise tugging at the grass a few feet away in the advancing dawn.. Several more tortoises, with shells the size of footballs, were moving past him over the sparse terrain. Rick rested on one elbow and watched them with wonder until they disappeared. He didn't tell the others about his tortoises. They were his secret.

TEHRAN, IRAN

JEN WROTE IN HER DIARY:

Win and I spent most of the day shopping in Tehran. It's very expensive, but I was naughty enough to buy a rug and a pair of earrings. Rudolf said he would change some money for me in one of the sinister little money shops, but Craig says he got a very bad rate of exchange. Tehran is a noisy city full of orange taxis and horrible Iranian men who not only follow you but pinch your legs. Win was very upset, but she would wear her shortest skirt! We picked up our mail from the post office. A letter from Mummy, and faithful Humphrey who says he will pay my fare if I ever want to fly back! I'm much too interested in travelling at the moment (and in you know who).

Two nights ago we were late for the customs coming into Iran so we camped by Mount Ararat. It was a beautiful white cone shape, you felt as though you could reach out and touch it. Quintin was beastly – he said there were poisonous trap-door spiders everywhere on the ground. Craig says we're very lucky to have seen Ararat because it's usually covered in cloud. By the time we had got through customs clouds were already there. It rained on the way to Tehran although we went through real desert! I walked away from the road and everything was completely quiet. For a moment I could literally hear the silence. But there always seem to be people about, even in the middle of nowhere: perhaps a little Persian boy with a few sheep, or an old peasant all by himself. They are more gentle and attractive than the Turks. And they don't wear those ghastly workers' hats: they have sheepskin caps, but the same ragged coats and trousers.

Tomorrow we are driving to Isfahan which Craig says is the most beautiful city in Persia. Rudolf is still extremely angry with C. He doesn't accept the decision not to see Persepolis, and he tries to get me onto his side. But I would rather see more of Isfahan.

ISFAHAN, CENTRAL IRAN

Rick stood outside the garage. In the distance were the turquoise domes and minarets of the city. The river ran under ancient bridges. Rick turned back to the workshop. The Land Rover sat on wooden blocks. An old man hammered with all his strength at one of the springs. Finally the small spring bush shot out and clattered on the concrete.

"Good!" encouraged Rick. He waited for the old man to pick himself up from the ground. The ancient grinned and flexed his muscles. Rick handed him the new spring bush and the hammering began again.

"It's got to be done bloody well," Craig had warned. "Tomorrow we're right out in the bush. And it'll be like that until we get to Quetta." Rick was impressed and made sure that the oil levels were checked accurately. The roof-rack was welded where it had begun to crack. All points were greased, and finally the vehicle was washed.

At noon, work stopped. Rick decided to explore the locality. He walked down a narrow street hemmed in by walls. Wooden doors led into bright courtyards. Above the street rode the dome of a church. A cross projected from the dome. Rick was curious to find Christians in Persia. He entered a paved courtyard. A bed stood in a corner of the yard. An old woman appeared in a doorway.

"Kreest?" she challenged. Rick nodded. He mimed the unlocking of a door.

"Can I have a look inside?" he asked. She went in and returned with a key. Shuffling across the yard in her long skirt the rotund woman rattled with the key. She turned it in the lock and entered ahead of the visitor. The interior was dark. Rick noticed rich murals under the dome. He saw several clocks. The ticking changed as he moved about the church. The woman coughed and crossed herself. Candles burned at the altar. A dark face of Christ scowled from the panels. Rick tried to concentrate on the paintings; but the woman shuffled towards the door.

"Kreest?" he asked, pointing at her.

"Ermeni," she said.

"Ah." Rick wandered through the district. He saw more churches. One had been built by a brother, he discovered, to spite the other brother's claim that he was the more devout Christian. It was an Armenian ghetto, clean and quiet, divided from the rest of the city by the river.

At the garage Rick found that no work had been done in his absence. He swore at the old man who smiled in reply. The old man resumed his hammering. Water had collected on the floor of the Land Rover, and the windows were steamed up. But the vehicle was clean. When the spring was refitted the back rode high off the ground unencumbered by the trailer. Rick was satisfied. He paid the bill and drove to his rendez-vous with Craig.

"But you don't want to look at all that crap now, do you?" discouraged Craig. "You can see the mosques and palaces next time round. Come and look at the shaking minarets." Val was indignant.

"Surely as Rick's been tied to the Land Rover all day he ought to be allowed to see what he likes in the evening."

"No, it's alright. I'll be coming here again," said Rick. "Let's go and shake up the minarets."

They drove to the famous mausoleum: two minarets linked by a single arch. Steve ran up the steps of one minaret, Rick up the other. Using their body weight they shook each minaret in turn which caused the other one to shake in sympathy. Steve became manic, gripping the tower as if he were Samson trying to pull down the temple. Both of them came down laughing helplessly.

Marshall and Quintin ran into each other as they walked back to the hotel. Each was carrying a large parcel. Quintin's bundle was square and heavy, Marshall's a giant disc wrapped in brown paper.

"It's a brass plate," he said, "only cost me fifteen bucks. Yours looks like a carpet."

"You're right," said Quintin. "And it's goddam heavy."

"Do you imagine these items will fit into the Land Rover?"

"If we keep quiet about them there should be no trouble. I'm going to stuff mine right up the front of the trailer."

"This plate may present more of a problem."

"Nothing a Chinese scholar and an expert in ballistics shouldn't be able to solve, I'm sure."

"I hope all the other idiots haven't bought stuff too."

"I suppose they're entitled to. But they don't all have the money."

The hotel was a cheap, modern establishment. The expedition was divided over three rooms. Marshall and Quintin ran upstairs and hid their purchases hastily under their beds.

"I saw ye!" hailed Steve across the landing. "Never mind. I got myself a brass dwarf. It's bloody big!"

Thomas was polishing some tiles which he had just bought.

"Christ!" he said. "How are we going to get all this junk on board?"

"Get rid of a few people," said Quintin.

"Yes, Rudolf for a start. He's a pain in the arse," said Thomas. "He's been following me about all day. Needs someone to hold his hand the whole time. No initiative, that's his trouble."

"He's coming up the stairs," said Simon.

"I say, I say, I say," said Edwardian Rudolf, rubbing his hands together. "What have folks got lined up for this evening?"

"A boot up the arse," mumbled Thomas.

"Where's Jen? I want to take her out to dinner."

"Blimey!"

"Ey sey, frightfully smart aren't we. We wants to take her out for a spot of dinnah!"

"She's in the shower," said Conrad.

"Good!" said Rudolf. He rubbed his hands together repeatedly.

"Why don't you rap on the door and pop the question?" said Quintin. "I'm sure she'll be delighted." He drew on a cigarette.

"What? No, I think I'll leave it for the moment actually. I've got a postcard or two to write." He rummaged in his duffle bag. US Marshall appeared at the door.

"Where's the General? Are we still supposed to be going to this smart restaurant tonight?"

"I imagine the Land Rover will be back very soon. Why, were you thinking of changing?" asked Quintin.

"I may put on some soft shoes. I guess my boots can skip their breaking-in program for an evening."

"Risky."

Marshall appeared dressed for the evening in his usual anorak, sweater and baggy trousers. A pair of brown shoes replaced his boots. The others welcomed the opportunity to dress up. Quintin wore a green silk shirt which reached his thighs. He complimented Simon on a leather jacket bought in Istanbul. Posh Jen wore a long skirt. Steve sported a red embroidered shirt and flared trousers. Edwardian Rudolf wore a linen jacket and a spotted bow tie.

When the Land Rover arrived Craig seemed shocked by their changed appearance.

"Pile in you rabble, we're going to my favourite restaurant." Win, the little Welsh woman, wondered whether Craig was in a good mood. He stopped the vehicle in a dark street and took them through a gate and a trellised garden to the restaurant. It looked like a private house, except that there was a bar in the corner of one room. The menus were written by hand, in Persian script. The restaurateur swallowed his indignation at their dress when he saw twelve people. They were ushered into a softly-lit room. There were no tables or chairs. They arranged themselves on the floor. At first they spoke in whispers. The menus were passed round; only one was written in English.

"Craig, what does this mean?"

"I don't know. I'm having a chateaubriand steak." Val tugged his arm and suggested that they have some wine. Together with Quintin, Jen and Thomas they ordered two bottles. Steve and Conrad wanted beer and beef stroganoff, with chips.

Two Persian couples watched from the other end of the room. The men wore dark suits, one woman a black trouser suit the other a satin dress. They seemed amused. They raised their glasses in salute. A musician entered. He was allowed to sit on a stool from which he sang wailing, incomprehensible songs. Northern Steve scraped his plate clean.

"That was bloody good," he said.

A dessert was brought in. The travellers fidgeted in an attempt to avoid indigestion. They sipped their coffee and tried to keep awake. The Persians were drinking dessert wine. They sent a glass filled to the brim to be tasted by the Europeans.

"It's like cough-mixture," said Steve. Thomas closed his eyes and let the liquor roll round his mouth.

"Full bodied," he opined. The Persians began to dance to the strange guitar music. They invited Rick, Steve and Jen to join them. One of the men, short and dapper, clicked his fingers and danced alone. He waved his body and stamped his feet, smiling at the prostrate English. He was attracted by Simon's blond hair. The Persian invited Simon to dance, but since he was refused, continued to dance alone, looking in Simon's direction for approval. He became the centre of attention. The other dancers made room for him; and he took off his jacket. As the music reached a crescendo, he stamped and clicked vigorously. All the diners began to click their fingers. At the final chord the Persian found himself in front of Simon. He drew the young Englishman up to his face in triumph and kissed him. The room burst into applause.

Rick was in conversation with one of the Persian girls. She spoke simple English. She gave him another glassful of their wine.

"You are Kreest?" she asked. Rick was surprised.

"Sometimes," he replied. The girl put a hand into her blouse and drew out a crucifix on a chain.

"I am Kreest."

"You must be Armenian. Ermeni?"

"Yes." Steve had also sat down with his dancing partner. He shouted across:

"Hey, Rick. How are you making out then? I wager we're gonna score tonight." He laughed and gulped his wine.

"What does your friend say?"

"He says you're very beautiful."

"He is *mast*."

"*Mast?*"

"He has much wine."

"Ah. Steve, you are *mast*." The news travelled round the room that Steve was *mast*. It was an expression which caused the Iranians much mirth.

"Perhaps it means more than we think it does." The bill was brought in. No one worried about the expense. The Persians paid for the wine. In the street the two parties said goodbye and got into their respective vehicles.

"So many in this tiny car?" said Sofya in wonder.

"There's room for you too." But she wouldn't come. Rick wanted her address but she would not listen to him. He was silent on the way to the hotel, while the others were exhilarated by their own company. Win vomited in the night.

SOUTHERN IRAN

Souvenirs were crammed into the overloaded Land Rover. The passengers sat tight for five days of desert crossing. The desert was relieved by towns at intervals: Nain, Yazd, Kerman, Zahedan, but most of their time was spent on rough roads winding through bare hills or looking across a waterless plain. After Yazd the tarmac ceased. Craig and Rick lowered the tyre pressures. They checked the wheel rims for cracks.

Quintin tried to read as they juddered over the corrugated road. He found that if he held the book in his hands, and forced his elbows down, *Middlemarch* vibrated at the same rate as his head. People's voices juddered as well.

"How's *Middlemarch*?" asked Jen.

"Absolutely gripping." The vibrations gave way to soft swishing when they drove over loose sand. Rick discovered that the vehicle behaved like a speed-boat, drifting round corners, swaying on the surface with the help of its four-wheel drive.

The oncoming lorries created minor sand-storms. All windows and vents were closed at once. Even then the dry smell of dust penetrated and settled. At sunset Rick left the road and drove a mile into the desert. He wanted to camp under the dark shape of a rock, but it was farther away than he thought. The ground was dotted with tufts of thorn, and scarred with channels - water courses which probably ran with rain once a decade. Rick switched off the engine, got out, and ran into the desert. After ten minutes the rock was no nearer. He stopped and stood with his hands on his hips while he recovered his breath. The red and saffron of the sunset was giving way to black. Rick waited until he could see the first star. He lowered his head and looked across at the small box of the Land Rover, now glowing with squares of light. He felt that it was very close. He could hear voices.

"Buggeration!" he said. He wanted the Armenian girl. He wanted Vibrant Val. He wanted something other than this bare desolation, beautiful though it was. "But you can't have it you stuck up bugger!" he told himself. "Bloody women." He walked back to the camp with long, easy strides. He imagined the muscles in his body as they took him smoothly back to the people. Twenty yards short, outside the circle of light, he studied the activities of his fellow travellers. Quintin and Vibrant Val were cooking. He imagined the warmth inside her thick sweater as she stooped over the pots. Surely there was a way of sharing her warmth. Cold bare legs and hotness above. Quintin – desolate, Quintin - looked beyond those things, unhampered by such madness; but he didn't look much further – to the scent of another man, perhaps. Beyond the Land Rover, Steve and Conrad played football with a tennis ball. Rudolf and Thomas had been playing too but, disappointed with their own lack of skill, stood aloof with their hands in their pockets. The others sat in the vehicle. They read, or wrote diaries. Marshall was crouched over a small piece of wood, knife in hand. Rick broke the ice.

"What are you making," he asked.

"A pair of chop-sticks. They're way more hygienic."

Marshall ate supper with his chop-sticks. When the coffee was made Craig brought out his bottle of whisky. He poured a dose of it into each cup. The travellers saw three large shapes about fifty yards away. They were motionless.

"What the hell are they?" said Conrad. Rick and Steve went to investigate. They saw three camels and two riders who sat as motionless as their beasts.

"Salaam," said Rick.

"Salaam," was the reply. The riders got down and began to collect thorns. Steve and Rick admired the haughty camels which stood in line like ships at anchor. Like engine rooms their stomachs steamed and rumbled. A stream of urine was jettisoned overboard. The riders lit a fire and threw tea-leaves into a pot. Their faces were red and wrinkled over the flames. Rick and Steve sat down with the laughing camel men and drank tea. They showed the men their watches. They examined the coarse woollen clothes that the men wore. One of them had a turquoise brooch which he wanted to sell. Conrad offered them a cup of whisky, which they drank, but not with relish. After an hour they strapped up their saddlebags and moved on westward.

Jen prepared to get into her sleeping bag. The stars shed a dull light over the desert, and on the dark shapes already spread on the ground. She rolled de-odorant under her armpits. She pushed her toes into the top of the bag.

"Jen." A shape was at her elbow. It was Thomas, the big, goofy teenager.

"Yes?"

"I wanted to ask you something." He held her arm and thrust his face close to hers.

"Go on."

"Whether you would find it possible to sleep with me. I mean whether you would ever let me."

"But Thomas!" she said gently.

"I know it's stupid to ask. But I've never, you know, felt so strongly before. Do you think you could ever bring yourself to?" Jen suppressed a laugh.

"Listen Thomas. Sleeping with someone isn't like that at all. You don't just ask them. You have to do it gradually, by little hints and things. Or - " she reflected for a moment. " - you have to sweep someone off their feet, suddenly and decisively, so that they can't say no."

"I suppose you can't make an exception just this once."

"No," said Jen. "What a strange boy you are."

"Maybe," said big Thomas, looking at the ground. "You won't tell anyone will you?"

"No. I promise."

"I'll see if I can do better next time." Thomas kissed Jen clumsily on the cheek-bone and retired.

Each town on their route was the same: dirt road gave way to tarmac. A roundabout, well ornamented with greenery and a statue of the Shah, led to the main shopping street. In the middle of the town the cross roads opened into a circus of shops, kebab houses, confectioners, wool merchants. City folk sported European suits and white shirts. There was no shortage of water. Coloured lights hung on the trees.

The travellers ate kebab on flat bread. They quenched their thirst with Pepsi-Cola from the numerous fridges. If there was a mosque to look at they gave it a cursory glance. Curious children gathered round the Land Rover. They peered through the windows at books and cameras. They imitated the mannerisms of the strange white people. Tongue was stuck out against tongue, fist shaken against fist. A policeman came to control the crowd while the travellers squeezed themselves back into the Land Rover. They were always glad to leave a town.

In the heat of the day they came from some barren hills onto a flat plain. Ahead of them was an acre of poplars, unbelievably green. Water ran down a polluted street. They came to Mahan, with its mausoleum to a Sufi poet. Few people flocked to pester them in front of the entrance. Two minarets shimmered above them in the sun. Through the archway a courtyard of cool marble heralded the spacious mausoleum. Quintin trod barefoot on the carpet of the interior. Light filtered through the marble grills. Two sarcophagi lay there in state. He might have spent an age in the deep gloom. But outside, the blond youth Simon was bathing his feet in a pool; sun glared from his shirt. Quintin left the mausoleum and walked along the pool, staring into the water. He stopped near Simon.

"It's the most beautiful thing I've ever seen," he said. Simon looked up at the mausoleum.

"I must say most Muslim architecture leaves me cold. But this has atmosphere. It really feels like a monastery."

"You like the idea of quiet asceticism being practised somewhere. Is that it?"

"Yes."

"Even if you don't lead a life of austerity yourself."

"Something like that. I've always admired people who do without things. I suppose the Middle Ages seem ascetic to us because they did without so many things which we regard as necessities." Quintin sank to his haunches.

"It gives one time to concentrate on the things that really matter."

"Could you become a monk?" asked Simon.

"I've got too many vices. And I'm very sensitive about them."

"What kind of vices: smoking, drinking, lechery?"

"Lechery of a kind." Quintin looked at Simon's shoulder. He put his hand on it. "But in some monasteries I suppose they overlook that kind of thing." Simon looked over his shoulder at Quintin.

"I wondered whether you might be like that. That's very sad. I'm sorry."

Quintin dropped his hand. He looked into the water.

"That's alright," he said.

Simon continued: "I've often wondered if there's anything I can do to help. But -."

"But what?"

"It always comes to the same thing."

"Go on."

"It feels alien to me."

"That's understandable. Do you believe in love between two men?"

"Theoretically, yes. Why not? But it's not for me." Steve and Conrad appeared at the other side of the pool. Steve tossed a pebble into the water.

"Fantastic place this," he said.

"Yuh, it's fantastic," said Conrad. Jen and Win came through a gateway at the end of the garden.

"Anyway, I appreciate your attempt to understand," said Quintin and stood up. Simon continued to wash his feet. He felt that Steve and Conrad, as they laughed, were laughing at him.

BAM, SOUTHERN IRAN

WIN WILTED in the heat of the afternoon, regretting that she wasn't losing weight. The Land Rover cabin was like an oven. Here, there were no sheds by the roadside with Pepsi signs painted on the walls. There was no greenery in the distance. It was pointless to stop. But Edwardian Rudolf complained that he would have to find a bush: he had diarrhoea. The passengers waited in the heat as he staggered behind an abandoned mud-hut. He came back again doing up his trousers, his movements were stiff and feeble, like those of an old man. Jen made a nest for him of sweaters and anoraks. He didn't say thank you but sank into the nest calling for water. US Marshall grudgingly took out his canteen.

"That's boiled water, fully sterilised," he said. "Don't let your lips touch the bottle, if you please." Rudolf gulped the water, spilling it on his shirt. Marshall held his hand ready to take the canteen away again. "That should be enough," he said. "He doesn't want to drink too much." Craig asked:

"OK?" in a bored voice, and they drove on.

The city of Bam suffered many sieges. In 1850 its inhabitants abandoned it and built a new town outside the gutted shell. But the walls of the old city still stood thirty feet high, and a citadel newly restored with bricks looked out over the plain against fresh invaders. In one corner of the enclosure the mosque was preserved, but the other buildings were only crusts of mud, arranged in honeycombs, purged of smells and people.

The Land Rover headlights picked out the mass of the wall against the empty sky.

"We'll have a look at it," said Craig. "I know a way up the wall." He switched off the lights and their eyes grew accustomed to the dark. A dog barked among the houses to their right as they walked to the foot of the wall.

"Right, synchronise watches," said Steve. Craig began to climb the dry mud face. He edged himself along until a fault ran up the side of the wall.

"This must have been made by rainwater," he said.

The more adventurous of them followed him up. At the most critical stage some steps had been cut into the mud. They heaved themselves through a gap onto the battlements.

"Careful," said Craig. "Some of the floor has caved in." They stood on a narrow rampart with a thirty-foot drop on each side.

"Bleeding hell," said Steve. He shone his torch into the gloom of the city. "I bet there's wild dogs in amongst that lot." By the far wall the citadel rose up above them.

"It gives me the creeps," said Rick. "Think of all those bodies put to the sword, and fires crackling everywhere."

"Oh don't!" said Jen. She had been brave enough to climb up.

"Nothing like a bit of burnt baby for breakfast," Steve grinned and winced as Jen hit him. He held her fists. Jen squealed with delight as she tried to free herself.

"Steve don't, it's dangerous!"

"You bet it's bloody dangerous."

Craig said "Hullo", in a knowing voice. The two new lovers struggled on the parapet.

"Steve, get off!" As the pair quietened down Val said softly to Craig:

"Cupid has struck." The others left the ramparts in silence. Jen and Steve came back later, helping each other down. That night in the desert they slept together, away from the rest.

Jen in her sleeping bag felt the angle of the rising sun increase. There was contentment in her which she could not have explained to Thomas - which made her sorry. Steve rolled over in his sleeping bag and found her face to kiss it.

"I'll fetch you some breakfast, lass," he said.

"That's not like you."

"I make exceptions for the daughters of gentlefolk."

"You, you have to bring your class war into the bed-chamber."

"That's where class wars are won," he said.

"Is that why you have taken me by storm?" She massaged his ribs.

"I'm a mean, calculating Scouser." He kissed her on the mouth. "Is that what they teach you at Benenden?"

"If you must know I went to a convent."

"Well I'll be buggered." Steve sat up in his sleeping bag and pulled on his shirt. He pulled on his trousers and walked over to the Land Rover.

"What's for breakfast then?"

"Good morning Stephen," said Win. "Did you sleep well?"

"Yes, yes. Anything left to eat?" Steve found two boiled eggs and some flat bread which he put on a plate. "Tea?" There was hardly a grunt to be heard.

"She has coffee," said Win.

"Oh," said Steve.

"No milk! And no sugar." Steve added the cups to the plate and stalked back to the bed-chamber.

"Christ! Don't 'ee go in among that lot. They eat you alive!"

"Don't they approve?"

"I'd be a liar if I pretended that they did."

"They'll get over it."

"Rudolf gave me a right going over. And Thomas looked like the harbinger of death."

"Poor Thomas. He's a very strange boy."

"He gives me the creeps. He stares at me as though I've knocked off his mother."

"Well you must be kind to him. Promise?"

"How can you be kind to an idiot like that? Give him a kick up the arse more like. 'We're all middle class nowadays,' he says, that's one of his gems. 'Quintin and ey are trying to conduct a meaningful dialogue' and Rudolf, he makes me cry: 'I think I'll take young Jen out for a spot of dinnah, Craig, *nota bene!*'"

"When did he say that?"

"Oh Isfahan. Didn't you know? He were all set to take you out, so he told us. But you were in the shower and he lost his nerve."

"Poor Rudolf."

"They've fallen for you like flies. You should be proud of yourself. They did a damn good job on you back at the drawing-board stage, my god yes. All the right ingredients."

"But the proof of the pudding is in the eating. Isn't it Steve. There's only one person who's allowed to eat me."

"And who might that be?"

"You." Steve tore himself away from her lips to eat his breakfast.

"Your coffee's getting cold," he said to Jen who was still on her back.

"Bam! I'll always remember this place."

MIRJAWEH, IRAN-PAKISTAN BORDER

In the afternoon they came to the customs post. The house was shaded by an extravagance of greenery and water fountains, although the desert lay all around and grey hills could be seen in the distance. The police official struggled to transcribe the twelve names into his book in Persian script. The travellers sheltered from the heat by a green pool and heard the crash of rubber stamp on passport.

"Pinish!" said the policeman. The expedition got to its feet and forced itself into the vehicle.

"Goodbye!" But there was still the military checkpoint a mile along the road, and the department of health.

After another hour the Land Rover took the road into no-man's-land, an eighty mile stretch between Iran and Pakistan. The evening descended early. Gusts of wind buffeted the vehicle sideways on the loose surface; sand drifted in spurs across the road, slowing the wheels at every encounter. Craig drove the car off the road into the desert and stopped.

"We're not going to camp here are we?" objected Rudolf.

"We haven't got much choice," said Craig. He opened the door and a blast of sand punched its way into the cabin.

MIRJAWEH, IRAN-PAKISTAN BORDER

"Christ! A real sandstorm," said Steve. He clapped Jen on the shoulder and she smiled. "Right! Volunteers to go out and dig latrines. Thomas!"

Rick forced his way out of a side door. Together he and Craig took the tents out of the trailer.

"Here, see if you can rig up some kind of a wind-break," said Craig. Marshall appeared by the trailer with the hood of his anorak firmly tightened round his head.

"Can I get my kitbag?" he asked. "I have a pair of sand-goggles in there." Marshall put on his goggles and attempted to pitch his tent.

They took Rudolf from his nest and laid him out on the leeward side of the Land Rover. He was protected to some extent by a wheel. The tarpaulin from the roof was hung on the windward side and bolstered with kitbags. Jen and Steve laid out their sleeping-bags under a thorn bush. They scooped up sand and set up their kitbags.

"Not much hanky-panky tonight then," said Steve. They slept with their backs to the wind.

In the morning the storm had ceased. Half a mile away fresh dunes glistened in the sun. The travellers shook sand out of their hair and clothing. They drank tea with sugar and sand. Rudolf thought it might be better if he rode in the front seat.

The expedition entered Pakistan. The customs post at Nokkundi consisted of a few shacks, a radio mast, and a railway halt. There was no food to be bought and no petrol. It was a day and a half to Quetta. They stopped at Nushki, the next town, and found some supplies. From there the road improved. They congratulated themselves on having got through the desert.

QUETTA, PAKISTAN

Lying on his bed at the government guest house in Quetta, Quintin wrote:

My dear Toby,
I am going through a kind of ordeal, self-imposed, from which I hope to emerge thrice burnished and thrice tempered, like Toledo steel. I told you of the exquisite blond youth who as early as Istanbul I hoped would crumble under the assaults of yours truly. I pursued him through Bithynia and Pontus, the cities of Rum, Tehran and Isfahan. Imagine my indignation when at dinner in Isfahan a dapper Persian in an expensive suit shoots his guard with one fell swoop, and scoops my beauty into his arms, kisses him indeed! What does the cherub do? He laughs. He wipes the saliva from his cheek and steals a glance – at me! Would you analyse that as encouragement?
In the desert his hair is the colour of the sun. Day and night I cannot rest. But like a scientist with his precious sample I hesitate to touch lest I destroy it with my rude thumb.
"Find a picture of Mahan, the only elaborate Muslim tomb I

have heard of. Envisage him by one of the dark pools scattered with petals and algae. We talk privately for the first time. And soon, discussing the pursuits of monks, I ask him whether he believes in love between two men: "Theoretically, yes. Why not?" he says. Exquisite modesty! I'm about to embark on a delicate circumlocution when a stone lands in the pool: the mirror is shattered: the Philistines are upon us. You can imagine I have hardly slept since. I ask myself what happened at Winchester?

We are now at Quetta. Still shaken by the rigours of a sandstorm two nights ago I have insisted on putting up at an hotel. The people are very civil. We have an army officer and an American oil man with us. The other "voyageurs" are camping in somebody's garden. My only companion in wealth is the American, Marshall B. Bronstein, a strange piece of transatlantic technology, who boils his drinking water for ten minutes every evening. That is not his only vice. He lives on vitamin pills and causes earthquakes with his Himalayan boots. What shall I do about the blond Simon? What would be best for him? I ask myself. Does the consummation of love always lead to corruption? That is my ordeal. To touch may be to destroy. 'Noli me tangere, for Caesar's I am.'

I could go on and bore you with accounts of the beauties we have seen. I could describe to you the shimmer of a blue ceramic dome floating on a mirage of tawny desert; the watered rose garden framed by a delicate stone fretwork in the Masjid-i-Shah at Esfahan; crumbling caravanserais situated nowhere, beyond which mountains are pencilled into the haze: but I will not. Suffice it for me to convey to you my tenderest wishes, considering it a privilege to sign myself your faithful brother in God, Q.

KABUL, AFGHANISTAN

"That's Craig," said Steve, "and that's Val." He watched the lion crouched in its pit. The lion looked out of its great bruised head straight in front at the wall. No thoughts went through its head. The furry body once primed for slaughter and supremacy was beginning to sag. A hunk of goat lay untouched by his left paw. Nudging his right, the flank of the lioness. She rolled on her back. She twisted her sleek head to look at the drunken head of the lion. She exposed the white underside of her belly. Her haunches cycled the air. There was no response from the lion. The lioness stretched herself in the sun; she licked her foreleg, reached round to straighten the hairs on her rump. All her actions proclaimed her body to be supple and ready for use.

"He's not having any, is he," said Steve. "What about this lot then?" He walked over to a walled pit which contained a dozen black pigs. "That's us," said Steve.

"They're the infidel," said Conrad. The pigs started at the sight of Steve and Conrad above the wall. They hustled to the other side of the pit, little creatures with pot bellies. But out of curiosity they felt their way back, heads rocking from side to side, letting out cautious grunts. Steve waited until he could touch the leader on the nose. He clouted it with his hand and let out a fierce yell. The pigs, without knowing why they were running, sped across the pit again and crashed into the wall.

"Who are the wolves?" asked Conrad. Steve screwed up his eyes as he watched the grey eyes of the animal. The wolf never stayed still. Its feet, each time they had crossed the cage, swung the body round while the eyes gazed constantly into the distance. All the weight of the beast was in its bolstered shoulders. The hind quarters tapered to nothing. The wolf was too rangy and long-sighted to deserve prison. "Quintin," said Steve.

"Jen is a giraffe, but they haven't got one here," continued Steve. They walked past the bird cages.

"And are you a giraffe too?" asked Conrad.

"No, I expect you would cast me as a bloody parrot! Look how many they've crammed in here. They're all on top of each other."

"Mebbe they had nowhere else to put them."

"And look at these owls. There must be forty of them in here. And they're all the same. What a rip-off."

"Perhaps they have a high mortality rate." An explosion cut through the morning air. Steve and Conrad looked about them. The zoo keepers in their shabby uniforms seemed as vacant as before. None of the birds flew up in fright. The deer in their plot of green continued feeding.

"It must be the Noon Gun," said Steve. They craned their heads up the crumbling hill above the zoo. Smoke cleared from a point at one end of the hill. "Are they up there?"

Win photographed the traces of smoke from the Noon Gun, and the view of Kabul behind it. The rocky hill on which the little Welsh girl stood, and the others that flanked the city, appeared to be crumbling into the plain. Only to the north were the mountains green and solid-looking.

"Kabul is a mess," said Marshall. He looked through his binoculars at the muddy river, the muddy streets and the pale plastered houses. "Like most of these Eastern capitals it has grown too fast for its drainage system. I hate to think of the pollution in that river."

"I'm sure they get used to it," said Win. "It's only the visitors who suffer."

"A capital that relies on foreign trade should first take care of its sanitation." To avoid Marshall's lecture, Quintin and Rick, followed by Thomas, began to descend the hill again. They took a taxi to the Khyber Restaurant. It was a large, modern eating house with a man at the door but self-service inside. Various types of European were collected there at lunch-time. At one table Val and Jen drank coffee while Craig looked over an insurance form.

"Hi," said Rick. But Thomas and Quintin sat down at another table. Rick followed them uncomfortably.

"We could be in London," said Quintin.

"In a ghastly office canteen," said Thomas.

"But this is a meeting-place of international repute," said Rick. "Everyone comes here on their way through. I suppose that's why it's so expensive." From the drinks counter they heard Conrad's voice.

"Hey, can I get a Budweiser?" He had seen some cans on the shelf behind the barman, but they were all empty. Steve paid for a tin of lager with his wad of torn notes.

"Bloody robbery," he said. They ambled into the main eating hall and joined Jen with Val and Craig. Craig looked up, then buried himself further into his insurance form. Jen's face became more animated. She was allowed a sip of Steve's beer. Steve had bought himself an Afghan waistcoat of badly cured sheep's hide. It padded out his slim torso. The girls sniffed at it and reeled backwards.

"Steve!" They held their noses. Craig scowled into his papers.

"It's positively lavatorial!" said Val. "You can't bring that into the Land Rover. Craig, order him to throw it away." Conrad's shoulders heaved as he looked at Craig. Craig did not look up but he said quietly:

"It might kill some of the other smells."

"What smells?" asked Val, she grinned at the others before nudging him. "What smells, Craig?"

"The smells of twelve people living in close confinement, that's all." Craig looked at Val, coldly.

"Win smells," said Conrad. "Christ, I don't think she ever bothers to wash."

"Shh! That's a very unkind thing to say," said Jen. "I'm sure we all smell a tiny bit after roughing it for so long." Steve sniffed under his armpits.

"You're right!" he said. "I'm beginning to decay. That's why I bought this coat."

"Don't be silly," said Jen.

"Silly? I'm being serious. You should smell my feet!"

"I probably have." She smiled at him.

"I think women have to take care of themselves more than men," said Conrad. "They don't seem to notice when men smell really high."

"You wanna bet?" cut in Val.

"But – " Conrad stopped. Val said:

"It sounds as if one of us girls has given Conrad a rude shock."

"Well, that's what I mean, you see, Win -."

"Val, I don't think we ought to let him go on," said Jen.

"We all know she stinks to high heaven," cut in Steve. "But

that's because she doesn't use all these fancy deodorants like you put on every night."

"You'd be very upset if I didn't!" said Jen.

"I like a fine natural woman," said Steve, bringing his fist onto the table. "With hair under the arms!"

"And hairy legs I suppose."

"Ay, I draw the line at a hairy chest, mind. But being a man of nature I can appreciate the beauty of natural ponginess."

"Well, all I can say is, either I'm a lot different than I think, or you've picked the wrong woman." Jen's voice was unexpectedly cold.

"Ahah, what's this?" said Val. "A lovers' tiff? I thought those were reserved for me and Craig."

Steve addressed Jen: "There's no need to look so cheesed off. It's not you I was talking about."

"Well if it wasn't me you had in mind no more need be said. You can go and find someone else who suits you better." Jen got up and walked away.

"I think I might have hurt her feelings," said Steve jovially.

"She's anal," said Conrad.

"She's what!?"

"Anal erotic. It means she has to clean herself up the whole time." Jen had reached the other end of the restaurant and sat down at a table alone. She opened her handbag and occupied her hands. She refused to look back the way she had come.

"You can't have it both ways," said Val. "Either you have the natural ponginess of Win, or you choose the anal eroticism of Jen."

"I don't like that word!" said Steve. "And which side do you fall on then my pretty maid?"

"That's not for me to say," said Val. "Ask Craig." She looked at him. "Craig, what -?"

"That's not for me to say either," said Craig gravely. He

looked up from his papers, and chewed the inside of his cheek. Val returned the stare.

"Steve, I think you'd better go and make the peace with Jen," said Val.

"What me!? I didn't start the thing."

"That's not the point. She's very fond of you. It means a lot to her what you think of her. So occasionally it would be nice if you showed a little appreciation instead of teasing her like that."

"Teasing her? I wasn't teasing her. We was simply having an intellectual discussion on women, wasn't we Conrad?"

"Right."

"And if her ladyship cannot take part in an intellectual way, then her ladyship must withdraw. Right?"

"Right." Steve fingered his can of beer and took a final swig.

"However," he continued, "under the circumstances I think it would be best to make the peace." Steve rose to his feet and ambled across the restaurant floor.

"There goes a real gentleman," said Val. Her chin was propped on one hand. She looked at Craig who was again buried in his papers. "It makes one feel very old," she said, "seeing them at that stage of an affair." Conrad grinned at her admiringly. She played to her audience. "When life becomes wholly decadent one doesn't bother about feelings like that anymore, does one Craig?"

"On the contrary, decadence is very hard, very precise work," said Craig. "The feelings have not vanished, they are twisted and channelled into something else. Ask Quintin, he'll tell you all about the art of decadence."

"But Quintin doesn't have any feelings."

"That's just where you're wrong. They may escape your superficial gaze, but that's because you don't know where to look for them." Craig leaned towards Val; Conrad could not hear him properly. "Under Quintin's melancholy good nature there is real turmoil. A turmoil that you and I can hardly dream of!"

"You're mad!" Val touched his arm and smiled. "Completely mad." She was delighted that her lover had become animated for a change. "Are we ever likely to see this other side of Quintin, boiling away?" she asked.

"Keep watch!" said Craig almost inaudibly. "Look and listen!"

Quintin had an uncanny feeling that he was being talked about. He could no longer listen to Thomas, who was expounding his theories on the writer Stephen Spender. Quintin stood up, pushing back his chair with a scraping noise.

"I'm just going to get some fags," he said. He walked to the entrance of the restaurant, not looking at Val and Craig's table.

"Do you think he heard us?" whispered Val.

"I don't think it's as simple as that," said Craig. Quintin stood at the entrance of the restaurant. There were cars parked in the space in front of him, two Land Rovers, an old Mercedes, a Toyota Land Cruiser. A young boy was cleaning the windscreen of the Toyota. Another ran up to Quintin.

"Wash your car, Mister?" He looked up at the Englishman, with his head craned right back. As Quintin took a pace forward he skipped out of the way and called again. "Mister, two Afghani!" The cigarette boy had spotted him. The youth, with a trayful of packets slung in front of him, hopped between the cars and offered "Marlboro cigarette, sir." He was taller than the other children. They crowded round him at the prospect of a sale. They laughed in a chorus of small, husky voices.

"Rothman's," said Quintin. "How much?" He put his hand in his pocket and felt a stack of heavy coins among some shredded notes.

"Sixty Afghani." The boy lifted out a blue and white packet. Quintin saw in the distance across the square the figures of

Rudolf and Simon. Rudolf walked with a bobbing gait beside Simon's even strides. Simon's anorak was open to the wind.

"Two packet one hundred Afghani," said the boy. Quintin found a one hundred note and stuffed the rest back into his pocket. He walked towards the Land Rover, hesitated, and lit a cigarette. One of the other children followed him eagerly.

"This your car, Mister?" Quintin ignored him and leaned against the front wing. "Your car washing very good." He looked at the windows of the restaurant. The reflection in the glass showed Simon and Rudolf advancing across the square.

Was he jealous of Rudolf? Where had they been together? He could not imagine that effete idiot having the wit to charm an intelligent boy like Simon. Could Rudolf make Simon laugh? That was the best criterion. He doubted it. On the other hand could Quintin make Simon laugh? When had he managed to do that?

"Mister you give me two Afghani?"

"Shut up!" Quintin jerked his head with rage but did not look at the boy. He tipped the ash from his cigarette. Could one ever do anything but laugh at Rudolf? The figures in the plate glass were joined by the real Rudolf and Simon. Simon was doing a silly walk, rocking from side to side. He laughed and simultaneously caught sight of Quintin smoking the cigarette. He spun round, and a tiny spasm passed over his face.

"Hullo," he said.

"Hullo," said Quintin. Rudolf gave an army salute. The door was opened by the doorman and the two of them went inside.

Now that Quintin was outside the restaurant he could not easily go in again. He could not see what was happening behind the plate glass; there were too many reflections. He did not want to sit at the same table. He did not want to face uncertainty, politeness, or ridicule. Was it so obvious to everyone that he was different? Or was everyone different from everyone else? You could argue the expedition was composed of twelve oddities. None of them was normal, none of them was trouble-free, each one of them probably had something to hide, some dark secret to be ashamed of! Quintin could not see them through the plate glass. But they could see him.

"What the hell!" he said to himself. He walked along the pavement. The eyes which he imagined were following him made his back judder. "What a place for this to happen," he said. "Persecution mania on the North-West Frontier." He threw his cigarette on the ground too far away to tread on it. "I suppose we'd better get some lunch," he said. He turned on his heel and walked to the door of the restaurant. The doorman had not noticed him. He was forced to push the door open himself.

LAHORE, PAKISTAN

Simon's diary:

Tuesday. We spent the night at the top of the Khyber Pass. This is because the border closes at sunset and we still had the Pakistan customs to get through. It's a fantastically eerie place. There are pill-boxes and gun emplacements everywhere on the Afghan side. The slits in the rock are like Mongolian eyes looking down on you. At the border we change from the tall, slouching Afghan soldiers in their grey denims to the smart khaki-clad Pakistanis. But the place where we spent the night was squalid. We slept on rush beds out in the open. They were outside a string of shops and tea-houses. Pakistani tea with milk boiled in it is disgusting, but I'm getting used to it. In these shops on the border you could buy anything from biscuits, to a watch-strap or a revolver. They were open all night. Wailing from a transistor radio was mingled with constant talking. A mangy dog slunk round our sleeping bags. The night was very mild; we could feel the warm air coming up from the Indus plain. In the morning the customs let us through first thing. We came down the hairpins of the pass into old India;

but photography was forbidden. It's magnificent to see such fertility after the bare plateau which we've been on since Turkey. I can see why India attracted conquerors like Alexander and the Moguls, and us! We stopped in Peshawar for shopping. I saw a cricket match at the Government High School, and newspapers in English! The military cantonment of Peshawar is just like Tidworth or Aldershot. In the suburbs of the town hundreds of people on bicycles. And Craig says this is only the beginning.

Thomas's diary:

Wednesday. If at any stage in our journey one could be said to have arrived, it is at the Park Luxury Hotel in Lahore. Although there are no peacocks strutting about on the lawns, parakeets in the trees do almost as well. The building, in two large sections, is graced with towers and verandas. A huge entrance hall and dining room. Bedroom suites with their own bathrooms. But everything is in an endearingly drab state of decay. Plaster floats gently from the walls. The carpets have resolved themselves into dusty grey matting. The dusty grey bearers perform every duty with a delayed action of at least half an hour. That is why sitting in the garden sipping one's gin and lime is liable to spin things out for a whole afternoon. Quintin and I have done our sightseeing for the day. Craig for once is getting himself grubby underneath the Land Rover – something to do with the brakes.

Perhaps this evening we shall take in another steak chateaubriand at the Salloos, excellent for the price of a dollar, followed by "Goodbye Mr Chips," at the Odeon, which our friend Stephen says is "rubbish".

. . .

In the garden beside Thomas, Quintin was reading *The Leopard*. He had bought it in a bookshop in the Mall.

"It's quite good," said Thomas, "but it strikes me as a rather complacent book. It makes the arrogant assumption that one can absorb change without pain."

"You don't think that's possible?"

"In life yes, but not in literature."

"Don't they try to be the same, as near as possible?"

"No. Literature explores not what *does* happen, but what *might* happen. It explores alternatives to the boring compromise that life actually is."

"Are you trying to say that life is reasonable, but literature is not?"

"Yes. To the extent that life works, but literature, being entirely in the mind, does not quite work. It's very near it, and it's clearer and more logical than life, but it does not work."

"Interesting."

"E.M. Forster. Vaguely."

"So no character in a novel is quite feasible."

"Quite. He doesn't exist."

The expedition was not alone at the Park Luxury Hotel. Drawn up by the lawns was a long bus with a kangaroo painted on the side, and the legend "Tuckerbag Travel"; Australians on their way down under. The bus was not working. It had already broken down in Kabul and now, with a crack in the engine block, it needed major repairs. They anticipated a fortnight's delay.

They said they had heard rumours of an accident in India, involving an English minibus. Three passengers had been killed, the rest had supposedly flown home either injured or shocked. Rudolf was indignant. He addressed Craig who stood with oily hands near the Land Rover.

"It proves that these drivers just aren't competent enough to cope with the problems of motoring in foreign countries. Their whole background is one of irresponsible, happy-go-lucky, hippie laxity. These tin-pot firms are mushrooming all over the place. They can't possibly know what sort of dross they are dealing with until the worst happens. And then they simply go into liquidation."

"You're right, of course," said Craig. "We just happen to be different."

"And what's to stop you colliding with a bullock cart at high speed, any more than anyone else?"

"Nothing. It's a risk we all have to take. If you're getting cold feet, now's the time to pull out. Of course there are no refunds at this stage."

"Scandalous! If the insurance companies knew what riff-raff were running these so-called expeditions they would never let them get off the ground."

"I've been in the game too long to take that remark personally," said Craig. However, he glared at Rudolf and picked up a spanner from the front wing. "In my opinion Rick and I can drive as safely as the next man. The only thing that's likely to happen is that we knock over an Indian. That's something the driver can't do much about. Sometimes they run in front of a car deliberately. But it's not going to be any skin off your nose if we do hit one."

"You seem to have a very callous attitude towards hitting Indians."

"I haven't hit one yet."

"But apparently it's just a matter of time before you do."

"Statistically, yes."

"You're nuts! You're a pack of gamblers – dicing with death." Rudolf hesitated: "Or rather other people's lives." Craig turned and shouted to Rick.

"Have you got that new wheel nut, Rick?"

"Yup," said Rick. He came round the side of the Land Rover.

"This gentleman," said Craig to Rick, "wants us to run over an Indian, so that he can prove how irresponsible we are."

"Sick. I don't like even to think about it."

Rudolf stood for some time with his hands in his pockets. He sauntered away towards Quintin and Thomas.

Marshall declined to go with the others to the cinema. He stayed in the hotel room which he was sharing with Conrad. Firstly, his boots had to be dubbined. He dusted his binoculars and his altimeter. He read a chapter of his book on survival in the tropics. From his briefcase he took out some airmail paper and began to write:

Dear Ignatius,

The quality of life in Pakistan appears to exceed that of the preceding countries. That is, the countries we have already passed through: Turkey, Iran, Afghanistan and including the two Communist states of Bulgaria and Yugoslavia. By quality I mean the presence of high-class foods, of bookshops and cultural centers and of facilities for English-speaking peoples.

Marshall unscrewed the top of his water canteen. He took two metal tubes from the breast pocket of his anorak and extracted a pill from each. Cupping them in his hand he shot them into his mouth, at the same time bringing the canteen to his lips. He swallowed three gulps of water. He replaced the tubes and screwed the top of the canteen back on. Marshall picked up his pen a second time.

. . .

This is not to say that the country is not in many respects desperately underdeveloped. I have seen no heavy industry. All highly technical products have foreign, that is, non-Pakistani trade names. There is little evidence as yet of Chinese infiltration into fields vital to the economy, except that I have encountered in Quetta, Peshawar, Rawalpindi and Lahore a number of Chinese restaurants. The proprietors on inquiry have proved to be either Formosans, Hong Kongis or in some cases not Chinese at all. Their attitude to a five-dollar bill precludes any possible suspicion that they might be Red.

Marshall got up again. He unstrapped his bedroll and took out a small hip-flask which had been wrapped inside it. Returning to his seat he flicked off the cap and put the narrow silver neck between his lips. He tossed his head back and felt the warmth of the whisky at the back of his mouth. He twisted the cap on again and stood the flask in front of him, opposite the canteen. He continued:

The plans for the Himalayan phase of the expedition are still not at all clear. It seems that the party will split into two groups, and each of the company representatives will take charge of a group. The object of the trek as laid down in the brochure is "to make a study of the traders coming from Tibet into Nepal via the Gandak river valley, particularly the nature of their loads, their character and their customs." It is already apparent that both groups will not be able to make the same survey. A splinter movement is anxious to go to a different part of Nepal altogether.

. . .

Marshall reached for the flask again. He rested back in his chair and tipped the flask almost vertically above his mouth. He came forward, rested the flask on the table, then repeated the operation. He resumed his writing:

I myself am considering a personal expedition of an entirely different nature.

He put down his pen and stood up. He paused for a moment in front of the table. He smiled for a second and went to the mirror. With his comb he smoothed down the short hair on the top of his head. He adjusted his spectacles. Marshall, armed with a pocketful of rupees went to the bar of the hotel. The room was almost empty. At a round table sitting alone was an Australian girl who had talked to Marshall that afternoon. She was writing a letter. Her left hand supported her chin.

"Hello," she said. She was blond-haired and strongly built, but she had a soft, relaxed manner.

"Hi, I'll just fix myself a drink," said Marshall. He stared at the bar, one hand playing with his pocket of rupees. There was complete silence. The barman was not behind the bar. Marshall turned to the girl.

"You writing a letter home?"

"Girl-friend in England actually."

"Uhuh!" Marshall smiled absent-mindedly at the girl.

"Excuse me, Sir." The barman was behind the bar.

"Er, Scotch whisky please." The barman poured out a measure.

"A big one. Thank you." Marshall took the drink to where the girl was sitting. He pulled a chair closer to the table and sat down. "We seem to have the place to ourselves," he said.

"Do you mind if I just go on with this letter? I'm almost through."

"Go ahead." Marshall clasped his hands together and leaned forward, his forearms resting on his knees. He studied the writing form of the girl.

"You decided against the film then," she said. She didn't look up.

"Pardon me?"

"You decided not to go to the film."

"Ah – no. I mean yuh, I did." He let out a short laugh. He leaned back in his chair and reached out for his whisky. He brought it to his lips and swallowed a small sip. He smiled. He exploded air through his mouth, and twisted the glass round in his hand, admiring it.

"There!" said the girl. She signed her letter with a flourish, folded it up and sealed the gum. All her writing materials were put back into her bag.

"I thought we might take a stroll around the town," said Marshall. He smiled thoughtfully at the girl.

"Aren't you going to buy me a drink first?" she said.

"Oh. Sure! What'll you have?" He rose to his feet.

"Same as you. Scotch, thank you." Marshall ordered a Scotch from the bar. The girl continued:

"You know, you hadn't struck me as being absent-minded before, but you are, very."

"I am?"

"You have a pre-occupied look about you." The barman brought the second whisky on a tray. Marshall did not look up but continued to stare at the girl.

"I am pre-occupied."

"Oh?" The girl's face lit up with amusement under the pressure of the stare. "And what might that pre-occupation be, may I ask?"

"A certain plan of action," said Marshall. "I have, for instance, a whole bottle of Scotch in my room. Would you be interested in partaking of a little?" The girl sipped from her glass, still looking at Marshall.

"Sounds like a good idea," she said. She drank her whisky with one gulp.

The hotel room was in semi-darkness. Light filtered from the veranda through the fly-mesh windows. Marshall's letter lay half-written on the table. A bottle of Scotch whisky threw its amber glow onto the wall. The electric punkah swung at low revolutions over the centre of the room. On one of the beds two forms, half-naked, sweated against each other. There was no speech. There was a sound of suction and grunting. The bodies were of no definable shape but moved in and out across the squares of light thrown from the window. It was not clear whether they were fighting or trying to perform a difficult feat together. The groans had about them an air of disappointment, or perhaps of calling for something that could never be attained. The speed of the action and the noise of the aggression increased, reached its climax, and slowed again. These climaxes were repeated several times. In the middle of the third or fourth climax Conrad entered the room. Before he was able to find the light switch he had noticed the shapes on the bed. He saw the squares of light changing shape on the bodies.

"Christ!" he said. Marshall's head twisted away from its work. "Excuse me," said Conrad. He backed through the door and closed it energetically behind him.

A day later, Marshall continued his letter to Ignatius:

. . .

My plan is to leave the main group when we reach the Himalayas and to conduct a trek of my own in the Everest region. I feel it essential, while it is so close at hand, to take a look at the highest mountain in the world.

"I may take a fellow countryman with me, a small, stout individual, not exactly my first choice, but he will have to do. We shall of course be fully equipped against the hazards of scrambling at altitude.

"At present we are waiting at the Indo/Pakistan border. There appears to be a certain amount of bureaucracy involved in the crossing. This is the only road open between Pakistan and India. It is not, as you would expect, the road which links Lahore with Amritsar, but one running considerably south of that to Ferozepur, obviously for defense reasons. The officials are not beyond reproach. I have seen them taking bribes. As yet I can see no sign of the alleged Russian influence on India, but we are after all only at the threshold.

At the border crossing there were children selling biscuits and bananas. Cold mango juice was brought from an ice-box. The leafy grove with a few buildings and tents seemed to be in the middle of peaceful countryside. Who could see that the fields two miles away were packed with military barriers and emplacements?

Conrad watched Marshall write his letter. He bit his thumb. It occurred to him that after four weeks with the American he did not know him at all. They had a plan to go to Everest together. But he was not a mountaineer. He had no desire to perform feats of endurance. He didn't have the equipment. Perhaps because he had seen Marshall in the act of fornication Marshall assumed that a dreadful intimacy had grown between them; that he had hypnotised him with his grinning stare.

Conrad looked at him nervously. He did not want to be bracketed with this fellow American.

As the sun set, a bugle call was blown and the green flag of Pakistan descended. The expedition climbed into the Land Rover and entered India.

At the next opportunity, Marshall continued his letter to Ignatius:

There is no immediate difference between India and Pakistan. The landscape remains the same, flat and heavily cultivated. There are fewer imported cars and more people. Ludhiana was a teeming mass of people and bicycles. We spent half an hour at a railroad crossing thronged by laughing, pushing Indians. The wallahs on their pedal rickshaws, tricycles with a painted canopy, are the most pathetic sight I have seen. Their bodies so undernourished hardly have the strength to propel them. And yet there is no aggression in these people. They do not go berserk, as I would have done in such a suffocation of numbers. The worst of it is that there is no prospect of them ever bettering their condition and climbing out of their environment. The Hindu religion forbids such aspirations.

The first ethnic group that we encountered, in western India, the Sikhs, seemed more impressive than the regular type of Indian we have seen since. They were tall, well-dressed and reasonably well-nourished; a proud people; the young men, not yet entitled to a turban, wearing their long hair tied in a knot at the crown. But as we head further towards Delhi the average stature and well-being of the population appears to deteriorate.

DELHI, INDIA

In Delhi the expedition bought food and other necessities for the Himalayan trek. Win was delighted with the capital. In the supermarkets and handicraft emporia of New Delhi she bought silks and sweet-meats. She drank iced coffee in the United Coffee House. She felt that she had at last discovered the joys of travel.

Quintin lay on his bed. The twelve were staying at the YMCA tourist hotel. A bible given by the Gideons was by the bed. From time to time the thwack of tennis balls outside impinged on his thoughts.

"Good clean-living, clean-limbed Christians," said Quintin - he was talking to himself silently, as he often did when he was alone. "Though their skins are dark their souls are as white as their cricket flannels – their smiles, the whites of their eyes." Quintin lifted one arm vertically and watched the unsteady progress of his finger across the ceiling. "While with us white men the corruption shows up on our bodies, our bruised, mottled pink flesh. Unless they are particularly immaculate, like Simon's." He dropped his arm suddenly. It hurt his thigh as it thumped onto the bedclothes.

"Women go blotchy when they are sexually aroused. I've never seen it, but I know it to be true." He looked at his forearm. He inspected the fine blonded hairs over the muscle. "Perhaps men do too." He sucked his forearm. "But then they have fewer erogenous zones. The blood doesn't run to their breasts. They don't have any!" He tried to imagine Simon with breasts. Would he find him attractive? "Disgusting!" He laughed and examined the traces of saliva on his arm. He saw spots where the blood had come through the pores. "What happens," he thought, "when you do that to an Indian?"

"One could always try," he said aloud. He surprised himself. His eyes looked round the room. Then he closed them and expelled air forcibly through his nostrils.

Another moment and his eyes sprang open. He heard activity in the room behind his head; his mouth opened, his heart began to pound while he listened. As well as the movements of Simon he heard the rushing of blood through his own body. Quintin sat up. He swung his feet off the bed and walked in his socks to the door. He opened it. Simon was humming to himself. It sounded as though he was unwrapping a parcel.

Quintin walked with care on the slippery linoleum. He found Simon's door half open and hung onto the handle as he entered the room. It annoyed him that he was breathing heavily.

"Oh, hullo," said Simon.

"Hullo." Quintin felt that, now he had seen Simon, his mind and body would be at ease. But his stomach tightened and dizziness overtook him. He could not let go of the door-handle. Simon looked up from the bed

"Hey. Are you alright?"

"Fine!" Quintin smiled thinly. "I'm just fine." He spun himself onto a chair near the door. "I just came to see what you were up to." He searched his mind. "You were making enough noise for a herd of elephants." He laughed.

"Oh, well. I've just bought these brass things. They look like wine glasses. I thought they might be very practical, a bit out of the ordinary, for dinner parties and things. They only cost me five dollars for six of them." Quintin stared at the goblets without saying a word. Simon shrugged his shoulders and continued cheerfully. "There's no limit to the stuff you can buy here. I wanted to get a beautifully inlaid table. And a painted brass chessboard. Are you sure you're alright?"

"Yes, carry on. I like hearing your voice. It does me a power of good." Another spasm passed over Simon's face. He looked down at his goblets and began to pack them up.

"I've got to go out again soon. I'm meeting the others at Gaylords, then we're going out to a flick." He looked up at Quintin. "Are you coming too?"

"Don't go," pleaded Quintin, "not this evening."

"Why? You're being very mysterious. Why not this evening? There's nothing else to do." He went on packing.

"Don't go," repeated Quintin. "It's my birthday, my mother's died, it's our wedding anniversary." He caught Simon by the wrists. "You mustn't leave me now."

"Look, cool it will you!" Simon wrenched himself free and backed to the window.

"I didn't mean to hurt you," said Quintin.

"You didn't hurt me. You're just behaving very strangely. You're not yourself."

"I am myself. It's you who are not yourself. You're beginning to blush."

"What are you trying to do? I've already told you that this sort of thing does nothing for me. You might as well be talking to a brick wall."

"A very beautiful brick wall. I can't believe that it has no effect on you at all."

"It does have an effect. But it's mainly – ." Simon broke off.

"Mainly what?"

"Something I can't share. I feel inadequate. You're wasting your time with me."

"Simon. No one would be wasting his time with you."

"I don't understand utterances like that. I try to understand them, but I can't. I wish I could, for your sake. But it's something deep down, physiological. You can't alter it."

"Simon. I'm not asking you to alter it. I'm asking you to be yourself. I'm being myself. I'm acting according to my instincts. Is it too much to ask you to act according to yours?"

"And if my instincts are to rush out of the room?"

"If they are. But then you're running away from yourself as well as from me."

"I don't see it that way."

"That's because you're conditioned. Ever since public school, and perhaps before, you've been instilled with a sense of guilt. What did you get up to at Winchester?" Simon shrugged.

"What about your friend on the other expedition? Just school chums?"

"I hardly knew him at school."

"But he knew you, didn't he. He knew you very well. I expect they talked about you in their sixth form studies."

"I couldn't help that. I'm trying to forget it. It happens to everyone."

"I find that difficult to believe. You have a charming way of leading people on."

"Oh do I? That's not proper queering anyway."

"What's proper queering?"

"Look. I don't want to go into this anymore. We're going to be living with each other for another two months."

"You don't want to understand, do you."

"No!" Simon began to put on his jacket. Quintin stood motionless.

"I see you've decided to run away from yourself," he said.

"I think it's the best thing for you as well as for me."

"Simon."

"Yes?" Quintin walked towards Simon and held him by the shoulder.

"I've managed this very badly. I'm sorry. I should respect that we are born under different stars." Simon smiled with an effort.

"That's alright. I feel terrible that I can't –," he turned away, "you know, reciprocate. It would be much easier." Quintin smiled; he had tears in his eyes.

"Now you make *me* feel terrible," he said.

"Well, anyway," said Simon, "I'm going to lock up." Quintin walked meekly out of the room. His mind was hurt by the rattling of the key. "See you," said Simon.

"See you." He watched Simon walk down the corridor and vanish down the stairs.

At Gaylords afternoon tea was being served. Like all Indian restaurants it was kept in gloom and the eyes needed time to adjust before studying the menu. Jen wanted cucumber sandwiches. Rudolf and Thomas insisted that the waiter produce muffins. They ordered two large pots of tea. The other customers eyed the group of tourists. Among the clientele were fat, well-dressed Sikhs wearing coloured turbans, leaning back in their chairs, and thinner more earnest Indians, some with spectacles, sitting forward over frugal cups of tea. In the darkness, which made it seem like evening already, a drummer and a pianist climbed onto the rostrum. They began to warm up. A pale-skinned woman with reddish hair and mid-length dress joined them. She adjusted the microphone stand.

"She's not going to sing, is she?" said Win.

"She's an Anglo-Indian," said Rick.

"But she's got a white skin!"

"They do have white skins. That's what Anglo-Indians are. They're very proud of it."

"But surely most of them must be illegitimate," said Rudolf.

"What a terrible thought!" said Steve. Jen turned to look at Simon. He was biting his lip.

"Simon. You're very quiet. Don't you want some sandwiches?" Simon looked at Jen for a moment. He touched Win on the arm and asked her for a cigarette. She had just been lighting one. She smiled and passed him the packet and her lighter.

"Thanks."

"We haven't seen this before," said Rick. The white lady began to sing. "Are you a secret smoker?" Simon shook his head, pretending that he couldn't hear. He smiled nervously and took his first few puffs in quick succession. Then he stared at the singer.

"I think someone's been trying to seduce him," said Rudolf to Rick in a low voice.

"Maybe."

The party left Gaylords and went to the cinema. After seeing the film they visited the Cellar discotheque. Coloured lights played on the walls. Western music filled the room with blocks of sound. The tables were crowded with well-dressed Indians and scruffy Europeans, all young people who didn't mix together.

"Bloody prohibition!" said Steve. "I'll have a Coke." Craig and Marshall were not present. The six men shared three girls between them. Thomas, hoping to talk to Jen, led her onto the floor but found that they could not hear each other above the music. Rudolf sat solemnly in a corner. He refused to drink Coca-Cola. He studied Val and Rick on the dance floor. They were enjoying themselves and the movements that they made.

They followed each other's eyes as their bodies flexed below. Rick wanted to hold the tough middle section of Val and stop it wriggling so provocatively. But she would not let him touch it. She held him all the time with her daring eyes.

Steve was talking to some Indians. They put a paper hat on his head, while Conrad and Win danced wildly to the music. Win had left Simon in charge of her handbag and cigarettes. Simon lit himself a third cigarette and found that his hand was trembling only slightly.

Rudolf decided that it was time to dance with Jen. He stepped onto the floor, his eyes blinking at the changing lights. He made a slight bow.

"I say, would you mind awfully if I had this next dance?"

"Not a bit, my dear man," said Thomas, "go ahead." He did a similar bow and left the floor.

Rudolf thought that he could perform a quickstep to the Caribbean rhythm. He thrust an arm into the small of Jen's back and caught her hand with the other arm, projecting it horizontally from the shoulder.

"Splendid!" he said. Jen returned his confiding smile. Pushing Win and Conrad out of the limelight the couple stepped in staccato fashion about the room. Win returned to her handbag feeling sorry for Simon.

"Come and have a dance, come on."

"I don't feel like it."

"It'll do you good, come on." Simon got up reluctantly and found that Win had already taken him by the hand. He screwed up his eyes under the glare of the lights and began to move. The music was so powerful that it seemed to punch his body. Win grabbed him by the wrist.

"I thought you were going to fall over," she said. Simon smiled. A frenzy overtook him. He tried to shake his body apart; he felt that he was expressing the agony of the human condition.

Win watched him with motherly concern, responding quietly to his extravagances. Simon danced until the club closed. They walked back to the hostel. The sweat dried on them in the night air. Simon felt the warmth of Win beside him. He kissed her under the dark trees by the entrance. They said goodnight in the corridor, but he dragged her into his room and fumbled with her on the bed. Win sat up.

"Simon! What's got into you? You'll regret it in the morning."

"I don't care about the morning. I must, I must." He began to kiss her again. Simon undid her bra and the zip of her jeans. Win lay on her back, half co-operating.

"Simon! I don't understand this."

"You must do," he said and tried to remove her jeans. But without Win's help the complications were huge. Simon lay half on top of Win. He remained still for ten minutes.

"I think I'd better go," said Win. She extricated herself from Simon; he groaned and lay still. Win closed the door softly behind her. When Thomas came to bed he wanted to tell Simon about the bar of the Hotel Imperial. But Simon was asleep in his clothes. He woke up at three o'clock, undressed and crawled into bed.

Quintin watched Rudolf dress himself in the morning. He saw him comb his hair, spreading it over the bald patch at the crown. Quintin lay on his bed, void of the will to get up. Rudolf put on his linen jacket and left the room. Quintin wondered whether he could face the members of the expedition that morning. What rumours had been circulating overnight? Their attitude to him must have suffered a terrible change.

He got up and took a long time over dressing himself. He combed his hair carefully. Quintin bought a paper from the room boy and began to read it before he reached the breakfast hall. He sat down at a table by himself. The waiter asked him whether he would like to join his companions. But he said he preferred to eat alone. Quintin hid behind his copy of *The Statesman*. He could not however avoid Rick's eye as he turned to another page. Rick smiled and looked back at Jen who was talking to him.

When he reached the toast stage Rick came across to Quintin's table.

"I don't think it's fair of you to have a whole pot of coffee to yourself," said Rick.

"That is part of the science of breakfasting alone," said Quintin. "But do join me in a cup." Rick sat down.

"I see you had boiled eggs. Very wise."

"It's the only way you can be sure of getting two whole eggs. With scrambled egg most of it's flour." Quintin found himself sweating under the strain of banal conversation. He stared at the paper.

"Anything interesting happened?" asked Rick. Quintin searched the page but found that he had taken none of it in. He felt Rick's eyes looking at him.

"No, nothing." He lifted his coffee cup with his right hand. As it approached his mouth it trembled so much that he put it down again. "Christ!" he said.

"Anything the matter?" Rick's face did not wear the mocking expression which Quintin expected when he looked up. The mouth was relaxed, the eyes fully open.

"Let's call it tooth-ache, shall we? I don't know whether I can face the world this morning."

"I think," mused Rick, "I know how you feel. But never mind. We've got the Taj coming up. That's what I call sublimation." Quintin twisted his face into a smile.

AGRA, INDIA

CRAIG SAT AT A TRESTLE TABLE. He thumbed through a battered paperback, *The Prime Of Miss Jean Brodie*.

"Aren't you coming to look at it now we've come all this way?" asked Val.

"No."

A moon hung over the shanty huts. Rick was waiting outside.

"Right. I'll go with Rick then," said Val. She stamped over the wooden boards of the restaurant. The door did not slam effectively. But she saw gentle Rick waiting to escort her. She forgot Craig back in the paraffin-lit room.

Behind the high wall the night-life of the wooden village hummed. But inside the second high wall and its Mogul towers, were gardens and long grass, symmetrical but containing luxurious shapes of trees and bushes.

The Taj Mahal was one step removed from reality, like a white ghost, the Platonic quintessence of all Muslim art, thought Rick. But if you walked closer to it you could detect flaws. The minarets were not straight. It was too big seen at close hand. They took off their shoes and visited the tomb. Shah

Jahan lay in the centre of the room; and the smaller sarcophagus of his wife, for whom the building had been built, was pushed to one side.

"You'd get a kick out of sleeping side by side in a place like this," said Rick, "even if you *were* dead!" They looked at the marble of the sarcophagi, mellowed with age.

"Let's go outside," said Val. They walked on the flat paving from which the four minarets rose. They stood where it overlooked the river Jamuna. A hundred feet below, the dark tide reflected the stars and the far lights of Agra. On the opposite bank were mudflats and flat fields.

"That's where he was going to build a mausoleum for himself, completely black," said Rick.

Val shivered: "How sinister."

"But the rising cost of living forced him to slum it in here with his wife."

"Cost of dying, you mean." Rick held Val's hair and kissed her on the side of the mouth.

"Oh!" she said.

"Don't you like it?" he asked.

"Well, I don't exactly abhor it." Rick thought he saw Rudolf. He guided Val into deeper shadow. He pressed her against the balustrade of the platform. Now, surely she would say stop, he thought. But he felt her tight muscles against his and she returned a kiss with ferocity. In a landscape of white stone they fought each other's flesh.

"And what about Craig?" asked Rick.

"Shut up. Keep doing it to me." Val leaned back and laid herself along the balustrade. On the other side was a drop of twenty feet. "Roll me over," she said. Rick felt that was a little public. He led Val down some steps into a garden. They crossed the lawns in bare feet: the grass soothing the soft soles. They stood under a tree and wrestled through their clothes. Rick twisted her onto the ground.

"You'll never get my clothes off now," she said.

"Perhaps I don't want to." He felt the warmth between her legs which he had thought about so much. He lay on top of her and massaged her through two layers of clothing. He ran his hands under her shirt and felt the warmth between her breasts. Rick went limp on top of her.

"Go on, lover boy."

"I can't," said Rick. "It's too complicated."

"It's more complicated for me than it is for you."

"No it isn't." He kissed Val and rolled onto his side, pulling her with him.

"Are we talking about the same thing?"

"People rarely do." She undid his belt and ran her hands over his stomach.

"Are you still sleeping with Craig?"

"Sometimes."

"Will you sleep with him after this evening?" Val gave a short laugh.

"I may do." Rick took her hand away from his stomach and turned his back on her. "What a jealous bugger you are!" Rick didn't reply. "I'll tell you what. I'll come trekking with you. I'll come in your group. I'm fed up with Craig." Rick turned back slowly.

"Ten to one you change your mind." Val knelt over Rick's face and kissed him on the lips.

"I promise," she said. Rick pulled her on top of him. "You've had enough," said Val. She got up and tucked in her shirt. Rick stood up.

"Ow!" he said. "Me balls."

. . .

Rudolf didn't see Val and Rick but he crept stealthily round the white ghost of the Taj. He saw Steve and Conrad in the gardens. He stood on the balustrade and watched them admire the moonlight on the white dome. He saw Jen come out of the burial chamber. She glided down the steps to where she had left her shoes. Rudolf descended another flight of steps. He fumbled in his pocket, approaching Jen as she stooped to find her sandals.

"I say, Jen, have you seen the river? It's absolutely ripping."

"No." She looked about her. She was ill at ease.

"Come and have a look." Rudolf steered her up the steps and across the marble plateau. He stood by her elbow at the balustrade.

"It's beautiful," she said. Rudolf fumbled in his pocket.

"Jen, I've been meaning to catch you alone for some time. During the course of this trip I have come to appreciate and admire you." Jen turned away.

"Rudolf," she interrupted. "Don't go on." She hung her head.

"Let me finish, please. I have admired you for your calm and your charity to everyone. Not least have I admired you for the way you put up with the insults from a person who likes to poke fun at your social background. I know you have affection for him, he's an attractive person. But -."

"Rudolf, I don't see any point in your going on. I – ."

"Let me finish! Think of your future. What will happen when you get back to England? Is this man going to have anything to show for himself? What is he? An office clerk from the north of England? What will your people have to say about that?"

"Really I don't see that you have any right to insult Steve in that way."

"Maybe not! But this concerns me in a way that you may not realise. Jen, when we get back to England I want you to marry me." Rudolf drew his hand out of his pocket. "You will forget this shoddy affair with a man so markedly different from you. And you will start a new life from the moment -."

"Stop! Stop! Can't you see how ridiculous this is?"

"I want you to wear this ring for me." Rudolf produced the ring triumphantly. Jen stared at him in amazement.

"You're like something out of the last century." Rudolf looked her in the eyes and tried to smile. "People don't live like that anymore," she added.

"Am I to take that as a refusal?" said Rudolf.

"I don't know what you'd better take it as."

"Very well, I shall ask you again." Rudolf took her hand. He went down on one knee. "Jennifer, will you marry me?"

"No."

"Oh." Rudolf stood up. He put his hands on the balustrade and looked into the night. "Why not?"

"I'm sorry Rudolf. It would probably be better if we didn't talk about it."

"Would you marry Steve?" Rudolf added: "*If* he asked you."

"I think we'd better get back to the others, don't you." Jen turned to go.

"Does that mean there's no hope of you ever changing your mind? I suppose it must have come as a bit of a surprise." Jen walked away from the river. Rudolf followed. Although he was very close to her, he didn't speak again. He put the ring in his pocket.

The four minarets guarded the shapely dome. As the tourists left the garden, the wooden gates were swung shut and locked. Behind the walls, in their marble bed, Shah Jahan and his wife were not bored with solitude. Their souls wandered through the garden over the tall grasses, under lascivious trees, in dalliance, imitating earthly lovers.

GRAND TRUNK ROAD, INDIA

THOMAS WROTE IN HIS DIARY:

Hindu temples are incredibly childish. I found one in a village by a lake. It was a little hovel with three rooms, and when I stepped inside I felt as though I had entered the youngest class of a primary school. Little papier maché idols were on the altar. A pink elephant! The best paintings of the term were stuck up on the wall. Various other bells and dolls lay scattered about. An old woman was sweeping out the temple. I pressed 50 paisa into her hand and made good my escape. I cannot understand Hinduism! I cannot understand Hindus. Since Agra it has been like one long suburb. Hundreds of people in twos, threes and sixes on bicycles, in pony traps, asleep on bullock carts, are littered aimlessly on the road. There is no room to pass them. Craig is very patient. All day we hear the sound of the horn. And woe betide us when we stop. A crowd of curious, inquisitive natives gathers round the car. They smile, they laugh among themselves. They make way for the great white sahib descending from his car, but then close around again persistently. There is no way of making them go away. They are not aggressive. Aggression has no effect on them. They smile all the more and want to make friends. Who wants ten million friends!

LUCKNOW, INDIA

Craig lay in his hotel bed waiting for sleep. Suddenly he saw Rudolf standing above him, hands in pockets.

"I shall be leaving the expedition tomorrow," said Rudolf.

"You what!?"

"I have considered my position, and I see that I can't continue under the strains which I am being subjected to at present."

"What strains? We're all under a strain at the moment."

"It's a combination of a lot of things. In addition to which I have put myself in a situation which you probably don't know about, and which you couldn't hope to understand."

"Do you mean your attitude to Jen?"

"Yes. I proposed marriage to her." Craig looked quizzically at Rudolf.

"I see. Did she take you seriously?"

"Absolutely. But she refused."

"You realise it was a pretty ludicrous thing to have done."

"It's only ludicrous in the context of this absurd expedition. We live like animals, and the women are treated like animals. In her proper surroundings a decent girl like Jen could not possibly tolerate the behaviour of a fellow like Steve. She would recognise him for the errand boy that he is."

"I see. You don't agree with crossing social boundaries?"

"Whether you like it or not, they exist. And when that girl gets back to civilisation she's going to regret her weak-mindedness."

"Hadn't you better stick around to bring her to her senses?"

"As far as I'm concerned it's too late. She's a fallen woman." Craig thought for a moment.

"If you believe that then I agree, every minute of every day must be torture to you."

"It is. And short of challenging the bounder to a duel I see only one course of action open to me."

"Honourable withdrawal."

"Precisely."

"You're a nutcase."

"What!?"

"A complete idiot." Rudolf stood rigid like a pole. Craig continued. "I've met some right ones on these trips, but you take the biscuit. You're bloody unique!" He laughed.

"But I say. I've been speaking to you in the strictest confidence. Man to man. I thought for a moment you might be enough of a gentleman to sympathise." Craig turned over. The laughter was still on his face.

"This is preposterous! Look. We've all had a rough time since Delhi. We've all got a heap of problems. Some are a bit more concrete than others. I suggest you sleep on it. And if you still hate us all in the morning we'll put you on a train."

"My mind's made up."

"We've almost arrived now. Once we're in Kathmandu you can lick your wounds in a hotel for a month. You don't have to be animals with us. Anyway, get some sleep. We all need it. We don't want to lose our ombudsman." Craig smiled.

"I suppose you're only doing your job," said Rudolf with scorn. "Goodnight." He walked into the garden.

BENARES, INDIA

THEY ARRIVED in Benares at sunrise. Craig parked in a crowded square near the river. Tradesmen of all sorts thronged the Land Rover. The bleary-eyed travellers got out and felt their faces cooled by the morning air. They trod carefully on the uneven ground and down muddy steps to the river.

Mother Ganges was a mile across, a huge conveyor-belt of milk mud, carrying dhows, rowing boats, dredgers, corpses and other refuse. She bore everything without a ripple to the sea.

They stepped into a small rowing boat with a single oarsman at the bows. His blades circled against the current and jerked the craft upstream. On the shore were washer folk at their laundry, slapping white linen against slabs of rock. Pof! Pof! The clean laundry lay drying on the mud.

Citizens of all ages washed in the river: fat senators, beautiful women, naked children, old hags. Some swam towards the boat. Others scooped up water in brass jugs and rinsed their mouths. Young girls let water soak through their sarees.

"How dignified they are," said Jen.

"Maybe the Roman Tiber was like this," said Quintin. They saw a dead cow floating a foot below the surface, and a dog with its body foully swollen. From the temples above, gongs summoned to prayer. A troop of monkeys skipped along the eaves. Young men were at exercise with wooden clubs. In the palaces lay the sick who had come to die.

A smell of charred bones came from the burning-ghat. Each body was wrapped in white cloth, tied to a wooden frame and scattered with flowers. After each fire the ashes were tipped close to the water's edge allowing the dogs to dig out any unburned flesh.

From the boat twenty yards offshore the city seemed an anachronism of dark stone, jumbled palaces and alien flesh. The boat was a time machine. It landed its passengers on the steps of the city. The tourists held their breath in the narrow streets, trying not to inhale any poisonous elements: even the scent of marigold petals warmed in the sun seemed unhealthy. They visited temples of gold and carved wood, temples harbouring cows and the smell of dung. The city was waking up. The shop doors opened, revealing merchants of thread and brassware, children selling flowers, sweets in wooden boxes, a pile of glistening jalebis.

Thomas bought a jalebi and crunched the sticky tubes in his mouth. He bought some bananas and fed the skins to a cow.

"This temple is replica of temple in Kathmandu," said an old monk. "You see a man and a woman, they make love. And here is man and two woman. This is two man, one woman. It is very good."

They had breakfast in a dark restaurant serving Western food, and ate hamburger steak. Thomas left the restaurant and walked through the streets alone. He saw jewellers, tailors in first-floor rooms, damp flagstones, brass pots full of water. The sun worked on the patches of earth open to its rays. He stepped around bipeds and donkeys. Indian boys ran after him. "Sahib, Sahib." Their dark eyes unnerved him. He saw the half-closed eyes of a beggar on a step. One fold of skin is like all other folds of skin, he thought. But it was a beggar's lifetime. He saw beautiful women born of mud, women suckling their young, dogs scavenging in twos and threes, old men on sticks. He could not look away, but he tried to avoid these pictures as if they were physical obstacles. He began to hurry, holding his breath for long intervals as if afraid to refill his lungs. He imagined the oxygen in the air had been replaced by Martian gas. These people were mocking him. He lashed out at a friendly touch on the arm. The smile of the beggar was the smile of his dead grandfather. He began to run. The air which he knew to be foul crashed into his lungs. There was no escape from this nightmare.

But suddenly, almost by accident, he found himself in the square and saw the Land Rover, beloved fragment of Solihull. Thomas gratefully took his place among his fellow aliens inside.

BODH GAYA, INDIA

Jen wrote in her diary:

Bodh Gaya is the first relief after seven days. It is like the first breath of the mountains and wide open spaces after the nightmare of the densely populated Ganges. We arrived in the morning when they were sweeping the temples. It was so peaceful; only the odd child, brought up under Buddha's wing, padded around the stones in his bare feet. The great boa tree murmured in the wind beneath the tall thumb shape of the main temple. A monk was at prayer, sliding himself up and down on a board, rather like doing press-ups. From the Tibetan temple we heard the clang of the huge prayer-wheel. It has to be pushed clockwise – anyone can push it. We looked at some Tibetan prayer books, wrapped in magenta cloth. The monks wear beautiful robes of the same colour. And at the gates of the temple some refugees from Tibet have set up camp. They gave us thupka, which are noodles, and Tibetan tea! made with salt and rancid butter in a long wooden churn. They didn't charge us for the tea. It was refreshing to see their broad Mongol faces. We really are getting near the Himalayas. I think everyone is feeling the relief. We certainly need at least a month before contemplating the drive across India again. I don't know how we contrived to hit only one Indian, and then only bruising his hand.

The Thai temple is very new, with a golden pagoda roof. I thought I'd forgotten what beauty and solitude were, until I sat there by myself for ten minutes; then walked back over the sheep fields. I felt completely refreshed.

DAMAN PASS, NEPAL

THE ROAD WOUND for six hours from the rain-forest of south Nepal, to Kathmandu, over the foothills of the Himalayas. The road circled tree-crested ridges, above little ribs of terraced fields worked by the Nepalese. They were tough, round-faced people; the women, sometimes naked to the waist, carried babies and baskets slung behind them from a headband. From the Daman pass, nine thousand feet high, the travellers saw the Himalayas for the first time.

The white peaks were fifty miles away. The ground between the peaks and Daman rolled full fifty miles, but the crust of ridges and glaciers was too high above the land to be convincing. Mountains could not be that high! They defied gravity: unless they were simply a backdrop made of cardboard, and painted cream to catch the sun.

"Somewhere up there George Mallory pissed into the snow," said Steve. Thomas and Rick ran to the top of the ridge where an observation tower had been built. They felt the scarcity of oxygen at nine thousand feet.

"I feel as though all my weight is in my boots," said Thomas. "My head's floating."

DAMAN PASS, NEPAL

"Like deep-sea diving," said Rick. The pair swayed as they studied what looked like a coral reef, eighty kilometres away. Everest lay hidden in a bank of cloud to the east. Annapurna in the west, where they were going, seemed an unexciting hump of white. Only one peak looked like a real mountain. It rose to a jagged point fluted with ice: Machapuchare, the Fish's Tail, just under twenty-three thousand feet.

The road descended again. The Himalayas sank beneath their foothills. Kathmandu Valley was broad and fertile, populated with Indian stock, busy with cattle and water-channels. The roads were filled with people. Kathmandu was a scar of concrete and mud on a valley of green.

KATHMANDU, NEPAL

Quintin wrote:

My dear Toby,
We are ensconced at the Withies Hotel on the fringes of Kathmandu. The proprietor is a handsome, well-fed Sikh. The Sikhs are known as the Jews of the East and Mr Withy is no exception. Before we even reached the city, one of his flunkies boarded the Land Rover and directed us to this doss-house. Of course there would be beds for twelve people, he promised - hot showers, laundry service, money-changing and information. Well, the beds were there. If they did not exist two hours ago they were invented with two boards and a passion. What larks! I am crammed into a room with our young Cambridge intellectual and the beautiful Simon. Plenty of scope for the wandering eye. The rest of the clientele is an assortment of hippies and Teutons in camper vans. The hotel costs five rupees a night, about half a crown, or less if you slum it on the floor of the two-rupee annex. You can even pitch your tent on the ten square feet of lawn. Meals may be ordered, but there is

no dining room. You either eat them outside, or have them brought to you like an invalid in bed. And then your tray always seems to lack the vital spoon or fork for eating your luke-warm egg. Showers are available in the early morning and in the evening. The water has to be pumped by hand into the roof. This is the job of Grandfather Withy, an old gentleman with a white beard. He has no proper quarters but sleeps on the sofa in the reception hall where he doubles up as night watchman. Among the hotel's other boasts is a beautiful view of the Himalayas. If you hoist yourself onto the flat roof and hang over the parapet you can just see the odd fleck of snow above the jumble of Katters.

But the virtues of the place must also be extolled. It is comfortably away from the throb of the metropolis. There is parking space, room to sort out the tents and baskets for the expedition. The Sikh is helpful, he speaks good English, he is always there, has a telephone, has a gorgeous wife. He works hard for his money.

Other rooms seem to exude a reek of hashish. But of course it's all legal in this country. You can buy cannabis in the Government Hash Emporium. A little boy no more than six years old touched me seductively on the arm and asked "Mister, you want some shit?" Western tastes are catered for in the little low-roomed restaurants rejoicing in such names as the Snow Man, The Hungry Eye, or Tashi's Trek Stop. There must be twenty of them in this small town trying to be a capital city. The menus include pancakes, peanut butter, apple fritters, chips and buffalo steak. Everything is cooked in a dingy back room on a paraffin stove, or scorched with charcoal. You can get porridge followed by egg and baked beans for breakfast, for a total of about two shillings. No wonder the hippies come and live here, spending their whole day moving from restaurant to restaurant eating a series of snacks.

The natives keep well away from these munching houses,

except for the complement of overfed, uncouth urchins who act as waiters, and the thin beggar children hovering outside the doors.

Beyond the temples and the royal palace is another world, the bazaar. We seem to be back in the throng of India except that some of the goods, and the people bringing them on donkeys and on their backs, are Tibetan. Their faces are Mongoloid, the blankets are of rough yak's hair. Sherpas buying food and equipment for expeditions walk like small bears among the thin, white-clad Caucasians. Some shops sell rope, and rucksacks, and the light reed baskets which are used for carrying everything in the mountains. The reeds should still be green when the baskets are bought, says our Sherpa. I haven't caught his name yet, it's a jabber of syllables falling over themselves among impossible "r" sounds.

We are to set off in two days' time. I abominate flying but the first eighty miles will be by aeroplane to Pokhara. There the groups will split up. (The CIA agent and his compatriot flunky are taking a tangent to Everest.) That leaves ten of us. Simon, the Cambridge man, and I are joined by Rick (the leader's 2i/c) and Val. Val was formerly the leader's sleeping partner, now turned loose. We five, as I say, we five are to attempt the long and boring route to Jomsom, the nearest an Englishman can get to Tibet. We have been issued with permits which allow us to go there and no farther.

The other five are attempting the Annapurna South Face, that is, they will walk to the base camp used by the 1970 expedition. Apparently you reach a bowl of mountains called the "Sanctuary", which is very beautiful. I shall be interested to see how Rudolf, the upper class twit, gets on with Jen, the horsey woman, to whom he proposed unsuccessfully at the Taj Mahal, and her lover Steve, the lad from the North. I imagine at twelve thousand feet the kapok will fly!

My own problems have hardly abated. But I will not upset

you with accounts of how I have been wrestling with my guardian angel and his.

You may feel that my mind is going. I am in excellent health. I shall provide you with a bulletin of our progress on foot in my next letter,

Yours in spades, Q.

After one night at the Withies Hotel, Marshall moved to other accommodation. He took Conrad with him. They paid five times as much and shared a double bedroom with wash-basin. From there, Marshall organised his private expedition. They were to fly to Lukla, where they would hire porters to take them to the Everest base camp. From the base camp they might mount a minor expedition of their own, perhaps scale a small peak of twenty thousand feet. Marshall insisted that they would need oxygen. He was told that he would get some at Lukla.

Conrad found satisfactory American food at the Nook, next door. He ordered himself a five-layer Neapolitan sandwich containing cheese, salad, hamburger, onion and carrot. Pancakes were washed down with a pot of coffee. He wished that the expedition were over. He needed to catch up on some civilised eating. This was a decent place; the room was clean; the showers were hot. Conrad strolled to the American library in town and read back copies of *Time* magazine. He read about his favourite football teams. He resented the earnest Nepalese studying newspapers from his own country.

Marshall and Conrad flew out of Kathmandu. Conrad looked the same size as his rucksack. In one hand he held an ice-axe. Marshall took a gulp from his hip-flask. His mouth set in a tight grin and his eyes remained fixed on the horizon. He took no notice of the gangway into the aeroplane. He took no notice of Val and Rick who had come to see him off. But he turned at the doorway of the plane.

"Goodbye you goddam Limeys!" he shouted brightly. He ducked his head as he entered the cabin of the DC3.

Thomas sat in the British Council Library, attempting the *Times* crossword. Other visitors rustled copies of the *Observer* or the *Listener*. He felt at home here, more than anywhere else in his travels. Even the luxury hotels of the Raj were full of mental discomforts; but in Kathmandu you could seek out an armchair here, or the corner of a little restaurant, and find that it was a small piece of England.

POKHARA, NEPAL

OVER THE NEXT two days Craig and Rick hired two Sherpa guides and ten porters. In the bazaar they bought baskets for the porters and other equipment needed for trekking. On the third day the little expedition of Sherpas, porters and Craig's trekking party of ten, boarded a DC3 bound for Pokhara. They sat along the fuselage facing inwards and grinned idiotically at each other as the plane took off. The only in-flight refreshment was a crate of oranges. After the thirty-minute flight the Dakota buzzed the airfield while a small herd of buffalo was cleared from the runway.

When the plane left again there was silence. They sorted out the baggage and divided it between the porters. As agreed, they would walk in two parties to different destinations: Craig, Win, Steve, Rudolf and Jen aimed to reach Annapurna base camp; while Rick, Val, Thomas, Simon and Quintin planned to follow the Gandak river to Jomson, a staging-post on the way into Tibet.

During the afternoon the two parties walked together out of Pokhara along the Seti river, past the Shining Hospital with its glinting metal roofs. Then their paths divided.

"See you in three weeks," said Rick.

"I hope not," said Steve.

Very soon the banter stopped as the Jomsom party faced its first hard ascent. The porters with their heavy loads chattered up ahead. At rest-points they eased the headbands off their foreheads and smoked their conical cigarettes. The Sherpa's face was already streaming with sweat.

"It's a sign of fitness," said Rudolf. "The Sherpas are a fantastic mountain people. Hillary would never have climbed Everest without Tenzing at his side."

By the time they reached their first camping place the tents were already up and the Sherpa had lit a fire. He made rice and curry with the cook boy. They chatted in low voices and often broke into chuckles. The porters had a fire of their own. They cooked tsampa dough for themselves, and joked in the fraternity of work and good wages. Rick contemplated them. He did not understand the machines that he had hired. What did they run on besides food and cigarettes? They had no cover for the night, except rough blankets. Some of them had no shoes. They worked like mules. They smiled under their loads. But would it last for three weeks? Large amounts of rice were brought on plates. Curry was poured on top. The Europeans ate until they could eat no more, the cook-boy and the Sherpa had the remains. As coffee was served the sky became pink. The snow on Annapurna became pink. Thomas stood up to observe the whole transition.

"Good God! There they are." He saw a blue tent a mile down the valley. It was pitched on a terraced field. A fire was burning. He could see Win's orange cape. But no sound drifted above the river's roar.

"So, they're giving us the cold shoulder are they," said Thomas. "Let's raid them at midnight."

"Burn their tents and rape their women," said Simon.

"You're welcome to them," said Rick. As darkness fell he felt closer to Val. In three weeks he would manage to tame her. Val spoke little. She was affected by the purity of the mountains. After the confusion of Craig and India, and of her own volatile personality, she wanted to start on a fresh page. Rick was a gentle being. He must not be allowed to rush her. She did not coax him like a cat. She let him kiss her cold cheek. She let him lie beside her looking up at the stars. The moon searched the slopes of Annapurna with its light. They listened to the murmur of the porters. Tsarong, the Sherpa, brought a paraffin lamp by which Thomas and Quintin were able to read.

Although it was only eight o'clock they went to sleep.

In the morning the cook-boy brought them tea. They watched the blue tent come down a mile away. They saw Win's orange cape, and the five ant-like porters already moving out of camp. Thomas was worried.

"Our porters haven't packed up yet," he said.

"It doesn't matter," said Rick. "We can start when we like. The cook-boy's the important one – he has to be ahead of us to get breakfast ready."

"So we might as well push on," said Thomas. The party of five set itself in motion. Simon's water bottle clunked at his waist, a sun-hat was tilted on his crown. Their limbs were stiff from the day before. They walked past a camp for Tibetan refugees, where prayer flags flew. They walked through a long village. The street was paved with flat stones. Cattle stood in the road. Little black pigs trotted from house to house. Cocks crowed, dogs barked, a prayer bell rang: the valley was not peaceful.

"Namashte!" They exchanged the greeting with every villager and every traveller they encountered.

Above the village, at a point where the path grew level, they stopped for breakfast. The sweat dried quickly on their backs. Soon familiar faces appeared over the brow of the hill.

"Oh no!" thought Thomas. "They've caught us up." The porters of both parties mingled and shared cigarettes. The women compared notes. The men were more reticent. Rick saw the two Sherpas chatting and wondered what they were saying.

"Our Sherpa Tsarong is extremely laconic," said Rick to Craig. "How about yours?"

"Likewise," said Craig. "It's quite normal."

"They're probably disappointed that they're not on some humungous Everest expedition. Tsarong has a faraway look in his eyes, even when he's speaking to me. Literally looks right through me sometimes."

The cook-boys were ready to move on. Both groups got up and slung on their bags and haversacks. They continued a little way together along the stony valley. Craig's group crossed to the right.

Tsarong and Rick's company began a slow ascent of the main path. They saw the others still on the valley bottom; and watched them begin a steep climb through the forest on the opposite side. Each group caught glimpses of the other across the valley, filing through the trees. As they grew tired, and farther apart, they lost interest in their rivals and set their minds on the next stop: lunch on the ridge.

BIRETHANTE, NEPAL

Quintin lay in his sleeping-bag at the mouth of a tent on the open hillside. Despite his tired limbs he could not get to sleep. The main impediment was a chorus of howling dogs answering each other from hillside to hillside. The long phrases were almost musical, but infuriating. One dog was so close to him that he heard its spiked collar rattle as it shook its head. This one seemed to be the ring-leader. Its long howls triggered replies from a mile, then two miles away, echoing around the valley. Anger seethed inside Quintin. This obstreperous animal needed to be taught some discipline! But the night air was cold. Quintin fumed for another ten minutes before finally galvanising himself into action.

"Right!" he said. He twisted out of the bag. He unstrapped his belt from his jeans and in his underpants trod across the stubble towards the dog. It stopped barking. As Quintin approached, it panted happily. He was furious. It had to bark before he could lash at it with his belt. He lashed at it anyway.

"Piss off!" he cried. The dog panted again. He stared at it in the speckled blackness. It knew no better. It was anxious to please. Quintin returned to the tent. As he settled in the warm down the dog began to bark again, a new song, from a different angle, with changed acoustics.

Simon wrote in his diary:

After Birethante we crossed the river and climbed directly for two thousand feet. The path is simply steps of uneven paving, sometimes loose, continuing the whole way up. After a quarter of an hour you are exhausted. We went on for breakfast at the top. This is the heart of Gurkha country. You sometimes see wizened old men wearing smart blazers with the Gurkha insignia. When they are retired they have to come back here and farm, which of course they know nothing about. So most of them do nothing except speak to tourists in their perfect English. The children are poorly clad and usually have runny noses and sores. The women are the amazing thing, carrying huge loads and singing and laughing as they overtake us. Our Sherpa Tsarong is first rate. He was with the Japanese on Dhaulagiri last spring. It seems that the Japanese are taking the place of British climbers in Nepal. Sherpas have made visits to Japan and physically the two races are far more similar. But the British are still respected here a good deal.

After breakfast we walked on to Ghorepani, climbing slightly the whole time. Then we entered the forest which continued up to the pass at about nine thousand feet. The forest is tropical, full of parakeets and monkeys. Grey monkeys with black tails swing in troops through the rhododendron forest. They keep their distance from man. The rhododendrons are not out yet, although buds are visible. Moving through the forest is like being at the bottom of the sea, mosses and ferns hang on the trunks, the leaves filter the light so that everything is tinged with green. We passed some spectacular pools and waterfalls. I don't know whether they're good subjects for photography, but I took some films.

Now and then we meet donkeys and pack-ponies driven by people who are obviously Tibetan. They wear embroidered boots and have long black hair in plaits. Their faces are creased and weather-beaten, like gypsies. They whistle to their animals all the time, a noise which blends with the din of their bells. Tsarong says he speaks a little Tibetan. Perhaps we can ask them what they are carrying, where they have come from and so on. What they think of the new regime in Tibet?

We are camped at Chitre. A little hut by itself with paddy fields to one side. It's still about eight thousand feet and cold as soon as the sun goes down. We're burning some bamboo to keep warm while the Sherpas use the proper fire to cook. We should reach the Kali Gandaki tomorrow. Then we follow the river valley to Tibet.

CHITRE, NEPAL

Rick stood beside Val. She was brushing her teeth. In the dark he studied the white foam dropping from her mouth. She drank from a canteen and spat water onto the mud. Rick waited for her to rinse her mouth again. She stood with her hands by her sides looking at him. Rick hesitated. He took the hand holding the toothbrush. The back of it was wet. He kissed Val. At the same time he wiped his hand on her sweater. She became soft, and hungry for more kisses. She dropped the canteen and put her toothbrush in Rick's pocket. Rick let a sob escape him. He kissed her eyes, nose and ears, under the jaw. He pressed his head against her neck.

"Why have you been holding out on me?" he asked.

"Have I?" Rick failed to understand her smile, so he kissed it out of shape. He took his head away to look at her again.

"What kind of answer is that?"

"You don't need an answer. Just hold me again." Rick obeyed at once.

"You're very cruel," he said.

"How can I be cruel? There's nothing to be cruel about."

"That," said Rick, almost to himself, "is the worst type of cruelty."

"The trouble with you is," said Val, "you want everything to be like a children's tea-party. Cakes and jellies, tears, forgiveness, nice surprise, more tears, then Mummy comes and takes you home. Right?"

"I don't see it."

"You can't face the reality of the world. Men and women, birth and death. As soon as things look black and ugly you think it must be wrong. You'd do anything to kill pain, weep and beg, or take a pill, shoot a horse."

"What's that got to do with you and me?"

"You only see half of it. You're always, as they say, going off at half cock."

"What?" Rick tensed. "Bloody hell!" He grabbed Val's arm and twisted it in a half-Nelson behind her back. "Pain you wanted, ey?"

"Yes." She hissed. He twisted further. "I mean no."

"What do you want me for?"

"I don't know."

"Some kind of substitute vibrator?"

"I say, that's rude. I didn't know you were a rude person."

"I'm not."

"Say some more, Rudi!"

"Shuddup." He kissed her hard on the mouth. They continued until they were out of breath. Rick studied Val again, panting. "Now perhaps we can talk."

"Don't talk to me, Rudi." They kissed for ten minutes. Because it was cold they entered the hut again. The others were still playing bridge.

. . .

Rick and Val dawdled on the path. They found flowers in the mosses. They found curious pebbles. The dust of the path smelled of donkey sweat. As the walkers passed them the donkeys stood to attention in their bright halters and saddle-packs. The bells nodded on the path behind them. They met water buffalo, soft-bodied, soft-eyed, swaying on their broad hooves. They saw porters bearing metal trunks. On a hillside they found tangerines growing in scanty trees. They bought some from an old woman. It was possible to see thirty miles towards Dhaulagiri, the world's seventh highest mountain. The main peak on the left spread a snow wing to the right, sweeping to a smaller point. Behind were the hills nearer Tibet. One or two clouds cast shadows on the waves of green and black. The light changed constantly.

"At school the sausages were fried the day before and heated in vast pans so that the skins went dry and crunchy. I love them like that," said Thomas.

"Chips thick and soggy drowned in vinegar, with a greasy slab of cod," said Simon.

"I prefer them thin with mushrooms and a nice bloody steak," said Thomas. "They do a very good one at the Turk's Head."

"That's a proletarian place."

"There's obviously something about institutional food which appeals when you're really hungry," said Quintin. "I remember seeing baked beans in an army kitchen being ladled out of huge tanks."

"I think it's just the notion of plenty," said Thomas.

"Would a boar's head interest you, or prawns in aspic?"

"I'd go for roast duck and orange sauce every time," said Simon.

"A friend of mine says his idea of bliss is sitting on a bog eating fish and chips," said Quintin.

"Perfect!" exclaimed Thomas.

"Absolute satisfaction regarding the two basic requirements of life."

"Commodious," said Thomas.

"Then what are we doing here?" asked Simon. "We might just as well be sitting on a bog in Battersea."

"We've come here to find out how much we really appreciate the comforts of life, like bogs," said Thomas.

"Let's open one of those big tins for lunch," said Simon. "Ham roll with egg."

"And we've got some mango chutney to go with it."

"And peanut butter," suggested Quintin. "I'm sure it goes well with your ghastly peanut butter."

"Or Marmite!"

Thomas mused: "I'm going to try it with everything. Lovely warm chapatis."

"Shuttup!"

LETE, NEPAL

THOMAS WROTE IN HIS DIARY:

We waited for an hour until Tsarong and the porters appeared. Tsarong explained that we had been going too fast; the porters were carrying big loads; we would have to slow down. There was no way of arguing. The porters sulked anxiously. Quintin in masterly fashion walked up to them à la inspecting officer and shook each of them firmly by one hand, while pressing a couple of cigarettes into the other. O loyalty cheaply bought!

After lunch we came to a place completely churned up by landslides. There is a kink in the river. Trees and stones have created a chute of loose earth down an eighty-degree slope. The crumbling path is shored up with tree-trunks. It seems that every year fresh disasters happen. But in compensation we had our first close-up of Dhaulagiri as we rounded a left-hand bend. It shone through a frame of pine trees; the peak high on the left, the confused ice-fall in the middle, and a wing of drifted snow inclining towards Tukuche Peak on the extreme right. The ice-

LETE, NEPAL

fall is where five Americans and two Nepalese were killed a year or two ago.

At this point the valley opens out. The river goes snaking off to the right. On a plateau inside the valley is Lete. It is an almost alpine village. Pine forests lie between it and the river. There are pine forests covering a small mound of two thousand feet which guards the way to Nilgiri. And pine forests again on the shoulder leading to Dhaulagiri. It seems a short walk to the summit.

We are staying at a house in the village. We have a room with piles of blankets, and a flat roof for star-gazing. Looking north you see no more giant mountains. The hills dampen down towards Tibet. It's a pity to be confined to this valley. I would like to go further afield. Perhaps we could make an excursion, at least the tough ones among us.

Quintin is not much of a walker, although he never seems to complain. I sometimes think I see the mask drop from his face and he becomes old and weary, fed up with self-propulsion. Simon on the other hand is full of keenness and the exploring spirit. But his legs are a bit short. I think when it came to the crunch we would have to leave him behind. By we I mean myself and Rick. He says he would like to spend a day seeing how high we could get. Leave the idle porters behind and take a few rations up to fifteen thousand feet or so. We must be at seven thousand to eight thousand already, on the valley bottom, and I don't feel any effects of oxygen scarcity. Rick spends a lot of his time dawdling with Val, but I think if it came to the crunch he would be capable of real effort. I'd like to do something spectacular now we're here.

Day 6

R and V made love last night. I heard them at the end of the room. The moans and gasps are very disturbing, until you almost wish, you would give anything to know that they weren't actually doing it, that it was all a show. The rest of us lay there as if we had noticed nothing.

LARJUNG, NEPAL

"Why don't we stay here for a few days," said Val. She lay on a flat roof in the sun, her hands clasped behind her head, in the village of Larjung.

"Amen to that," said Quintin. "We've been on the go for six days. This is technically the weekend." Thomas said nothing, but he cut into the mud roof with his sheath-knife.

"It's about time we talked to some Tibetan traders," said Simon. "That's what we came here for."

"That's a load of bull," said Thomas. "We'd need a proper interpreter and we'd have to be here about two months before we learned anything at all. As far as I'm concerned we've come here to see the country."

"Exactly," said Val, "to *see* the country. That doesn't mean rushing through it at breakneck speed. There should be time to look about us. Then we might learn something about these Tibetan traders, whatever they are."

"You don't want to go to Jomsom then?"

"No."

"Rick says it's just a couple of huts and a handful of soldiers," said Quintin, "and then you turn round."

"But he doesn't know does he. He hasn't been there. You want to get to Jomsom don't you Rick?"

"I'm afraid I do." Rick looked at Val who said "Huh."

"On the other hand –."

"Come on. You mustn't let yourself be swayed by your concubine," said Thomas.

Rick looked at Thomas sharply. Val laughed.

"That's a long word for a little boy," she said.

"We all heard you last night," said Thomas. "And we think it's disgusting."

"Oh do we?" said Val. Thomas glowed red. There was a silence. Simon broke it quietly.

"Really, I'm not sure I know what you're talking about. I slept like a log."

"So did I!" said Rick. He stood up. "Well! I think it's time we marched on, don't you?"

"God!" said Thomas. He descended the ladder from the flat roof and walked ahead of the others.

"I wonder what's bitten him," said Simon to Quintin.

"Adolescence."

Larjung village was on the west side of the river. The river bed was a mile across, a desert of pebbles with a few arms of the river arching through it. Small dust storms blew along the flat plain. Larjung lay two miles below the ice-fall of Dhaulagiri. In between were yak pastures. A Buddhist temple stood on a promontory, a square pagoda. Some caves were carved into the cliff and painted two-tone red and cream, like the houses. At the end of the village stood another temple. Simon and Quintin were invited to look at it. A series of prayer wheels stood to be rung by those who entered. Simon ran his hands along them.

"Like the rollers of a conveyor belt," he said. Inside the dark temple the walls were covered with paintings. As the walkers' eyes became accustomed to the gloom they saw in more detail the horrifying composite beasts and dragons, lions with bird's heads, snakes, elephants, griffins clutching babies. The colours were fierce and glossy on a background of green.

"So this is what it's all about," said Quintin.

"If they believe in that lot I'm surprised they can get a night's sleep," said Simon.

"Some of these are their friends."

"It's a much better view of the world really, with good and evil mixed up."

"Who's this bloke in a football jersey?"

"Harry Krishna." They returned to the glare of sunlight, the glare from the dust on the river bed, and from the snow.

"Tremendous vitality," said Quintin. "It's what everybody fears and wants to paint."

"And they put it in a temple."

"They cram the motive force of life into a little box."

"It's difficult to believe in good and evil being at large in these mountains," said Simon.

"Why?"

"Because everything is so much regulated by the seasons and the animals. There isn't time to be wicked. What evils can these people do to each other?"

"I think we'd be surprised." Quintin and Simon came to the river bed. They walked on the loose pebbles. Dust flew in squadrons up the valley. Ahead were Val and Rick. Now and then they bent down to pick up a pebble.

"We've found a fossil," said Val. "Believe it or not this place used to be covered by the sea." She handed a stone to Simon.

"It's a sea shell!" he said. "You wouldn't believe it, we must be at about six thousand feet." He handed it to Quintin. "D'you think there are any more? Simon began to examine the pebbles. "I'd love to get hold of one."

LARJUNG, NEPAL

"We'll find one for you," said Val. The four walkers continued with their heads bent to the ground.

Thomas watched them from his vantage point. He was on the hill path used in the monsoon. From a shoulder of rock he looked down to the river bed.

"Bastards!" he said. They were frustrating the first great experience of his life. "Inconsiderate bastards!" Tears came into his eyes. He pitied all previous men of vision. History was full of them, pioneers choked by the inertia of others. "Rick's got no grip," he decided. He hit the rock with his fist. He knew they were talking about him down there. Far worse, he knew that they were not giving him a moment's thought. "Unmitigated fools!" What were they looking at? Some item of time-wasting trivia. They would never rise above the excrement of their own mediocrity. No, not even Quintin.

Thomas saw the shadow of an eagle flash over the rubble. Or was it a vulture? He saw the bird wheeling a stone's throw from the rock. Now and then it rose vertically without effort, now and then it rowed itself with heavy strokes to another thermal.

"That's what I'd like to be," Thomas decided. Alone, rejected, and elevated. The great bustard. He watched its feathers like fingers playing delicately with the wind; the tail twisted up and down in an expert slalom. "I'll be one of those, please," he said to his god. The eagle became a small speck against the hill. Thomas sat motionless for a long time. He stared at the vortex of Nilgiri across the valley: rock and snow twisted into a Roman amphitheatre. Above it, crags and ridges. An Everest expedition found a dead eagle at twenty-eight thousand feet. "I'd like to go up there," said Thomas in scorn of the human race. "I'd like to go high."

. . .

"From such fools mountain climbers are born," said Quintin. "Did you notice Thomas has been reading John Masters?"

"What's wrong with John Masters?" protested Simon.

"Ah," said Quintin. "It's difficult to say."

"You're being mysterious again." Quintin felt a pain in the stomach.

"Don't you sometimes wish the whole of the British Empire had passed us by?"

"Emphatically not," said Simon.

"We would then treat the people and places we visited with some kind of respect, instead of trying to conquer them in one way or another."

"We gave up conquering years ago."

"Did we? But we still have a patronising manner when we address foreigners, as if we were still their masters," said Quintin.

"It's what they expect of us."

"And they don't begrudge it?"

"No. It doesn't mean anything. It's just a charade that's played out on both sides. The word 'sahib' for instance doesn't mean they think we're superior. It's just convenient to call us that."

"To flatter us and get money out of us," said Quintin.

"If they can do that then they deserve our money."

"Anyway thank heavens we're passing the buck to the Americans."

"God forbid! They have no idea how to handle people," said Simon.

"Ah! Thine own mouth condemneth thee, o pukka sahib." Quintin wanted to kiss the wounded face of Simon. His motives were the basest of all. Worse than a conqueror, he was a subverter. But it was enough for him that he could talk to Simon. He had not damaged their ability to get on. They talked sensibly. They had so much in common. It would be senseless to destroy the balance with an ill-timed kiss.

"What are you thinking about?" Quintin asked softly. Simon's face twisted for a second.

"Bombay actually."

"What about Bombay? Your sister? That you won't have to put up with us for much longer?"

"No." Simon's voice was quiet.

"What then, Simon?" Quintin came too close.

"Leave me alone! Go and bother someone else will you!" Simon stood stock still. "Go away, please."

"I'm sorry." Quintin turned and walked ahead of Simon. He did not look at the ground. His feet stumbled once or twice against the pebbles.

TUKUCHE, NEPAL

THE HOUSE at Tukuche was built round a courtyard. Steps led up to a flat roof. On the side which faced the street there was a second floor, a long dark room. A paraffin light burned. Thomas, Rick, Simon and Val played bridge. Quintin sat against the wall. He did not read. His hands were clasped in his lap, his legs extended, one crossed over the other. He did not smoke.

The matting creaked as the bridge-players shifted position. Simon had indigestion after a large supper. Thomas hummed to himself and shouted: "Double!" He was happy after a talk with Rick. Tomorrow they would reach Jomsom.

"Fuck," said Thomas, to show that he was happy. "I have boobed." The faces glowed in the lamplight. Rick looked intently at his cards. He ignored Val's attempts to tickle his feet.

"You're taking this far too seriously," said Val.

"It's your lead," prompted Rick.

"Oh, anyone would think we were playing for money." She flung down a card. Simon laid out his hand on the matting.

"Nice," said Rick, "we'll have the two."

"You realise you're vulnerable and doubled," said Thomas. He lashed down with his ace.

Rick didn't take his eye from his own hand.

"Of course," he said. He produced the three of trumps. Simon collected the trick. "First blood to me," said Rick. He played another trump. Simon as dummy was unemployed. He got up and walked through the doorway. He heard cattle stamping in the courtyard below. From the edge of the flat roof he heard the rush of the river; he thrilled at the brightness of the stars over the snows. But he was also aware of the little doorway on the ground floor. Yellow fire flickered from it. There was the clank of pots. Laughter followed soft, rapid voices. A baby cried. The cattle stamped again. From the long dormitory there was no noise. Thomas said "Damn!" in a rising voice. Silence again. Simon imagined the warm hearth below stairs, the round faces of the women, and the creased face of the cook-boy.

He returned to his bridge hand. Quintin was already in his sleeping bag, lying with his hands clasped behind his head.

JOMSOM, NEPAL

THOMAS WROTE IN HIS DIARY:

Today we reached Jomsom! Very undramatic but it was worth it. After Tukuche we came to Marpha, a village nestling under crumbling cliffs punctuated with scrub. The going has been mostly flat since Lete. But we were away from the maddening pebbles of the river bed. The wind got up. Dust blew in our faces. It's really desert from now on. The hills have little vegetation, they are heavily eroded and sandy coloured. As we came over the rise we saw a long sweep towards Jomsom. Three miles across the valley was Thini and what looked like a monastery built on a rock. There is an air-strip before Jomsom, rough earth cleared of stones. And the wreck of an aircraft lies at the end of it. Canadian. We walked up to it, the door was banging in the wind. It had been stripped of everything. Half of a wing remained. We might be on the Tibetan plateau already, everything is so desolate and open after the gorge we have just come through. We see little clusters of dzos or mules, two miles away, in a ball of dust, being driven towards us. Eventually they pass us and we study for a moment the dark Tibetan faces, black hair and red boots.

Jomsom is just a military check-post, a few huts, a couple of soldiers, and several large furry dogs. The main village is across the river, but we can't be bothered to go and see it. We have our trekking permits stamped by the soldiers. We eat lunch. And we are on our way back again. This is the climax of the whole journey, the goal which we embarked on from London. It seems an anti-climax. Perhaps it won't be, looking back on it.

MARPHA, NEPAL

"Bloody hell!" Rick clawed at a creature which attacked his long hair. His hands triggered off a clattering of bones and the stench of death. "Do they have to hang their dried meat in the bedrooms?" He bent his head to avoid the sticks of rib. It was cold. He undressed quickly and slid into his sleeping bag. He turned to kiss Val goodnight.

"Stay with us tomorrow," she pleaded.

"No."

"I'll be bored without you."

"Thomas and I want to go high."

"I'll come too."

"You wouldn't last five minutes. Look, you rest tomorrow, alright?"

"Alright," said Val. "Make love to me."

"No. We've got to get up early."

"Right!" Val turned her back. She lay still.

"Val." Rick touched her shoulder, but she didn't respond. He kissed her ear and went to sleep.

The cook-boy brought porridge to the three mountaineers.

MARPHA, NEPAL

Dawn was hardly visible. The stars were blown from the mountains by a sharp wind. When they had eaten, and packed their lunch, the cook-boy led them up the slopes of scree behind the houses of Marpha.

It was natural to feel exhausted after the first quarter of an hour.

"Got up too early," panted Rick. "Sugar level in the blood needs," he drew a breath, "time to rise."

"Crap," said Thomas. He was tired but he kept going at a steady pace. He never varied the rhythm of his steps. He wheezed a song in a heavy, sticky tempo. Thomas would not be the first to give in.

The cook-boy led the way fifty yards ahead. There was no expression on his old-young face. They had discovered his name today: Pemba. He carried the lunch in a linen bag. Simon was last. To show his indifference he stopped to take a photograph.

The base of the valley was like the sea: the flat roofs of the village formed a little port. But already the climbers felt closer to the slopes of Nilgiri across the valley. They saw tough pine trees flattened into the slope. The whole surface seemed to consist of loose chippings. Once, they found water, a trickle out of dry rock dampening a few stones on its way down. As the sun rose the air was no warmer. But they felt its rays on the back of the head. Marpha was out of sight behind the shoulder. After three thousand feet they reached the top of the shoulder. The landscape changed. Here were bushes and pastures, rocks growing out of the turf. The slopes leaned back into a green bowl. There were huts, abandoned in winter. In proportion, like gigantic downland, this pocket runnel of Dhaulagiri swept to a head of seventeen thousand feet.

"D'you think we can make it up there?" said Thomas. "It doesn't look very far."

"Let's have a rest," said Rick. They stopped and considered the top of the bowl. Patches of snow were visible on the last thousand feet.

"It would be good to get to the snow-line," said Rick.

"From the top you should see Tukuche Peak." Simon joined them. He drank from his water bottle. They noticed that he was panting with shallow breaths.

"Simon, I think you ought to rest," said Thomas.

"You go on," said Simon. "I'll catch you up."

"Why don't you wait for us here?" said Rick. Thomas saw that they could get on more quickly without Simon.

"We could come back for a late lunch. In fact we can leave our lunch here with you and make a lightning bid for the summit."

They found a large rock. Simon lay under a bush nearby. Pemba sat down as well.

"You not come, Pemba?"

"No." Thomas and Rick saw themselves in a new guise. They were the mad British climbers who took Sherpas with them to the limit of their endurance, and then went on alone.

"Very well then."

"*À bientôt.*" Rick and Thomas had a water bottle between them, and some sweets. They set off along the springy turf. The ground was almost flat.

"Where is everybody? These are supposed to be yak pastures."

"Hibernating." As the sides of the bowl climbed steeply again Rick and Thomas followed a rising contour of their own. They crossed the scar of the main stream coming from the snows. From that point their course was more vertical. The surface was still covered with grass, thick and tufted, the rocks were more frequent.

It was difficult to breathe. When they rested, even after ten minutes their breath was not regular. They sucked a sweet, drank some water and turned to face the slope again. Although their limbs were heavy their heads swam in a menthol atmosphere.

"We'll rest for ten minutes," said Rick, "then we'll try to get to that rock up there." The rock was only sixty feet higher. When they got to it they had to rest again.

"We must be nearly sixteen thousand feet up." They reached the snow. Thomas kicked his way into it and sank up to his waist. They picked their way between the patches of snow.

The ridge which led to the summit seemed within their grasp.

"We've got another hour, then we have to turn back," said Rick.

"We should do it easily." They rested ten minutes and climbed for five before resting again.

"I can't believe it," said Thomas. "We can't do any more. It's pathetic." They aimed for rocks only thirty feet above them, then rested some more. "Let's have another sweet."

"I can't breathe with a sweet in my mouth." Rick blew phlegm out of his nose. Their movements were reduced to a third of normal speed. Across the valley Nilgiri seemed about the same height. They were level with its snows. They felt for the first time equal to the vortex of rock and ice. They saw the mountain in its true proportions, no longer a thick-booted giant, but a lion with a gigantic head and mane of snow.

The sweat dried on them. They looked down the way they had come and felt weak.

"We'll never make it down there."

"What you call a knee-trembler."

"Photograph!" Thomas lurched from his seat and set his camera. "Will you take one of me?"

"Yes, if you take one of me." When they had each fumbled with the shutter they sat down again.

"Right, we'd better go," said Rick. They drank the last of the water.

"We can melt some snow," said Thomas. He crammed some wet crystals into the mouth of the canteen. Rick let himself jog down the slope. The muscles above his knees ached. His back and his head ached. It was impossible to be nimble, but they kept upright on the steep descent. They descended fast. It hurt them more to go slowly.

"The rock!" said Thomas. They saw the rock where Simon and Pemba were waiting.

"I wonder if they saw us." As they jogged into the bowl the lion of Nilgiri turned up its nose. It withdrew the grandeur of its upper slopes. The Roman amphitheatre became a flat dish. Because of the change in air pressure they could not hear properly. The pastures of the bowl were silent. They heard only their own breathing and their own voices.

"You were very quick," said Simon.

"Christ! Did you see us?"

"No. I've been asleep."

"Have some genuine snow."

Thomas wished again that he was an eagle. From the shoulder it was a three thousand-foot drop to the village. Every foot of it had to be gripped and controlled by the soles of his boots. At each jerk a knee caught his weight and released it again until the joints were like burning rope. Lack of oxygen gave him a headache. His spinal column and all his nerves shocked at each contact with the ground. The ground crumbled and crashed away from his feet.

Reaching the paving of the village street was like entering a dream. He floated into the house. His muscles twisted him up the steps, to the dormitory room, to the dried meat.

"Bloody hell," Rick murmured. He let the brittle ribs play with his hair. "Time to go to bed," he said.

Val looked up from her book. "But it's only three o'clock."

EINKO CAVE, ANNAPURNA, NEPAL

CRAIG TROD in the footsteps of the Sherpa. Fresh snow had fallen overnight: the surface came above his knees. It was like riding a heavy bicycle. Steve toiled behind him, taking deep, easy breaths. Norbu swung his ice-axe above the level of the snow. Occasionally he thrust it in to steady himself. They came to a river of jumbled ice, a small glacier. Norbu tested it with his ice-axe, then he swung himself across the frozen lumps. The walkers followed.

At the valley bottom a stream broke its way through the snow. The walkers heard it rushing out of sight.

"Annapurna Sanctuary," said Norbu. He pointed his axe. The clouds were heavy, but for a moment they poured away, leaving a sunlit ice-wall visible beyond the sides of the valley.

"That must be Annapurna Three or Four or something," said Steve.

"Here's another avalanche." A cloud of snow shot from a ridge high to the left. Bundles of rock and snow rolled across the path two hundred yards ahead. "This is getting dangerous," said Craig. Norbu grinned.

"Should we go on?" asked Craig.

"If you wan' we can go," said Norbu.

"Very comforting." More snow thundered onto the path. It continued like an express train for twenty seconds. Steam rose from the rubble.

"We'd better go," said Craig. Norbu glissaded on his ice-axe. Craig and Steve stumbled after him. They retreated down the valley. As they reached the cave the clouds closed in and it began to rain. Jen and Win stood in the cave. Rudolf lay in his sleeping bag. A fire was burning. The porters, some barefoot, huddled on a ledge higher up. This was their day of rest while the white sahibs climbed the mountain. It was only three o'clock and the white sahibs had returned.

"Time for a game of cards," said Steve. He took off his woollen cap and shook his hair. "Christ, the bloody porters have nicked the cards again." Pasang brought some tea. Jen and Steve sat next to Rudolf. They looked out of the cave. Banks of cloud rolled up the valley, obscuring the other side. The cave was called Einko. It was not really a cave but a jutting slab, protecting a triangular space, open on two sides. The wind funnelled through.

"What did you see up there?" asked Rudolf.

"Two yetis and a one-eyed camel," said Steve.

"You might have waited for me," complained Rudolf.

"We did, but then we thought you'd given up. We couldn't hang about all day."

"I was only having a pee."

"Bloody long pee. Anyway we kept looking back and you didn't show up, so we went on, heart-breaking as it was."

"I'm sure."

"Rudolf turned up here looking very po-faced. He hasn't said a word all day," said Jen.

"Poor old Rudi-chops. Never mind, at least you've had a

chance to dry out. Win, come and sit the other side of me, I'm bloody frozen!"

"Oh my gawd!" said Rudolf weakly. "At least keep your foul boots off my sleeping bag."

"This is nice and cosy. Orgy time!" Steve pulled the girls closer to him.

Craig stood by the fire. The snow had melted inside his boots. He felt warm water between his toes. He heard an avalanche across the valley. Behind the cloud came the cracking of rocks. He heard the muffle of snow. Craig unlaced his boots. He wrung out his socks and held them over the fire. From the kettle near the fire he poured himself another cup of tea.

Pasang and Norbu had already begun to prepare supper. The climbers were hungry after their attempt. A packet of dried curry was emptied into a pot. Rudolf found it more difficult to read. He closed his book. He drew his sleeping bag round him, so that only nose and moustache peered out.

After supper the walkers drank cocoa. They took the cards from the porters and played a round of poker.

"Well, we were defeated by the mountain," said Craig.

"Beaten before we started," prompted Steve. They spent their second night in the cave.

In the morning the expedition returned down the valley. It was three days' march to the main path. They met no one. Most of the track led through forest and bamboo. They saw little besides the enclosed valley. Clouds covered Annapurna behind them. For a moment they saw Machapuchare, the Fish's Tail, almost on top of them, above the valley shoulder. It had never seemed so huge. They could make out individual ribs of ice. They were awestruck by the vertical sweep to both peaks.

"It's terrifying," said Steve. "You don't need any film music to make you scared stiff."

"People must be incredibly brave, or incredibly unimaginative, to climb things like that," said Craig.

"Or they are driven by an insane passion beyond our comprehension," countered Rudolf.

"Well, that's one mountain that hasn't been deflowered," said Craig, "at least not properly."

Descending the valley they covered in two days the distance that had taken three days to climb. They spent the first night in Chomrong, a village cupped between the main gorge and a subsidiary one. It was a basin of tidy fields surrounded by crags choked with greenery. Jen admired the slow life of the water buffalo. She stared at the large eyes, rolling timidly below the submissive slant of the neck. She wanted to stroke the vulnerable nose.

"I can't believe they'd ever harm anyone," said Jen.

"Devilish brutes!" said Steve. "Batter you to death soon as look at you." A child with a runny nose beat the buffalos on with a stick.

"Buff steak!" he continued. "That's what I'm looking forward to in Kathmandu. Buff steak and chips for three rupees. A nice hank off the shoulder there, lovely."

"Poor thing! I expect that's where they all end up."

"In the bellies of the rich in Kathmandu. All the natives eat is dhal and rice." But it was not true. In the evening a porter came to the house chuckling. He carried an armful of red meat. The lady of the house took the meat and cut it finely with her knife. She fried it in a pan, and when it was brown tipped it into a large pot. The porters squatted in the shadow back from the fire. There was no chimney and smoke filled the room. The porters after four days in the cold, some of them barefoot, looked forward to a portion of meat.

The English were driven out by the smoke onto the veranda. They sat on rush matting and played cards.

Win, the little Welsh woman, was fit. She felt happy. Colour stayed in her cheeks, she knew that her black hair had become glossy. Short legs did not affect her performance. Since the second day, when she had climbed two thousand feet with great difficulty, her limbs had become attuned to mountain life.

"It must be the Welsh woman in me," she said. "I'm really a little mountain goat." As they left Chomrong she walked jauntily in front of Craig.

Only Edwardian Rudolf, like an old man, rolled his sleeping bag painfully, and followed them from the veranda, dragging his feet. He stumbled on the rough paving of the village street. His face was pale and deeply lined. His thin frame seemed to crawl sideways out of the village. He stopped frequently to drink water. The walkers waited for Rudolf at the top of the first climb.

"How's it going?" asked Craig.

"It's terrible, quite terrible," said Rudolf. "I must have dysentery or mountain sickness. I feel so desperately weak, like a little baby."

"What about the blisters?"

"Bad." Rudolf blinked at the four faces. He read in them either sympathy or disgust: he was not sure.

"Well, we can't carry you, so you'll have to come along as best you can," said Craig.

"I don't want to be carried," muttered Rudolf, "It's just this blessed stomach pain." Steve played with a walking stick which a porter had cut for him. He whistled loudly to himself.

"See you at lunchtime," he said. Win followed his long strides down the path with her solid little steps. Jen stayed behind with Craig and Rudolf. She had guilt feelings about his illness: that it might be a product of unrequited love.

"Have another pink pill," she said.

"I've already taken three this morning."

"Have another one."

"Well, I'll leave you to it," said Craig. He hesitated for a moment then swung round to follow the others.

"You've hardly got any water left, have some of mine," said Jen.

"Thank you." Jen put the pills into her haversack. She felt her arm caught in a desperate grasp, as of a dying man.

"Is your answer still no?" she heard. She looked into Rudolf's pale eyes, ringed with darkness.

"I've told you once and for all that it's no." She removed Rudolf's hand. "Now put it out of your mind or you'll make yourself even iller." Jen stood up and shouldered her haversack.

"I'm sick with love for you."

"Nonsense. Now get up and pull yourself together or I'll leave you behind." Rudolf didn't move. "You're dribbling! You're like a little child." Jen took out her handkerchief. "Here, wipe your mouth." But she had to do it for him. "Get up," she said. Rudolf groaned and turned his head.

"Oh I'm so alone," he said.

"Get up for heaven's sake." Tears came into her eyes. "Get up damn you." She tried to pull Rudolf up by the arm.

"Haha memsahib." Two of the porters appeared on the path. They were amused by the antics of the white lady.

"Help me!" she shouted. They laughed again and disappeared into the forest.

"Right! I'm going to leave you here to die." Rudolf closed his eyes.

"Alright," he said quietly. Jen moved away. She looked back. Rudolf had not stirred. She walked five minutes and then stopped. She waited ten minutes until she saw Rudolf on the far shoulder of the hill. He moved like a zombie, one foot rocked forward and took the weight from the other. He looked neither to right or left. He walked past Jen without noticing her. Rudolf sat by himself at lunchtime. On the turf by the broad stream he rested his head on his knees. They brought him food but he ate little.

"It would be fine if my condition was improving," he said, "but it obviously isn't. I suppose the insurance doesn't cover such a trivial ailment as chronic amoebic dysentery."

"I suppose you want us to lay on an air lift," said Craig, "with nurses from St Thomas's."

"They do have a helicopter don't they?"

"Only three hundred dollars."

"At the moment I'm not doing anyone any good. I'm holding you all up.

"No you're not, you're doing fine." Rudolf looked cynically into Craig's eyes:

"I'm not that gullible, Craig. I know you're dying to see the back of me.

"Nonsense, we enjoy having you around."

"Well, in that case I shall disappoint you."

"And how do you plan to do that?"

"I shall be leaving the trek at Ghandruk. I'll find my own way back to Kathmandu."

Craig replied quietly:

"Splendid." He walked back to the others.

In the evening they reached Ghandruk. As before, they spent the night in the village school. It sat on a promontory overlooking the steep gorge. On the other side of the gorge, a mile away as the crow flies, but half a day's march down and up, lay the village of Landrung.

"That's your way back," said Craig.

"It should be pretty simple, considering it's the way we came," answered Rudolf.

"You'll have a porter with you: we're sacking old Chimney Chops. He'll take your kitbag back to Pokhara."

"And who may I ask is Chimney Chops?"

"Does it matter? He's the one who smokes a lot." Rudolf left in the morning before the others had packed up. His face wore a new mask of determination.

"Good god! He's looking almost human," said Steve.

"If I am it's because I'm seeing the last of you. Goodbye!" They watched Rudolf move with short paces down the hill. Chimney Chops padded after him, his basket bouncing because it was so light.

"Poor old Rudi-chops," said Steve. They were in a jesting mood. "Nice little foursome we've got here. Bit o' sex, bit o' fun and games, eh!" He slapped Win on the rump.

After the first mile of walking they were serious again. Sweat and toil demanded attention. There was no Rudolf to slow them down and set them at ease.

"I hope he'll be alright," said Jen at lunch.

"We shouldn't have let him go," said Win. "He might get a stomach cramp."

"Why didn't one of you go with him then?" said Steve.

"Craig said he'd be alright on his own."

"And so he will," said Craig. "His illness was due to an overdose of self-pity."

"And what about the blisters?" objected Win.

"He'll be alright."

GHANDRUK, NEPAL

THE GROUPS of Rick and Craig met.

"What have you done with Rudolf?" asked Rick.

"Oh, he had to go back. Terrible stomach pains."

"Predictable. We seem to have kept in pretty good shape."

"I didn't expect to see you this far down," said Craig.

"Well, we got to Jomsom, rested a few days here and there, and suddenly everyone wants to get back. How far did you get?"

"We had to turn back because of avalanches."

"Sounds pretty hairy."

"So we're going to see how far we can go up your route before heading for home."

"Fair enough. What was the highest you got."

"Only about twelve thousand feet. We were up to here in snow."

"Tom and I got to nearly seventeen thousand, didn't we Thomas?"

"That's right."

"Well, be seeing you."

"OK."

"Good luck," said Rick. His party swaggered on.

GHANDRUK, NEPAL

. . .

Thomas wrote in his diary:

I realised, at that moment, that what I am doing now is only a remote fraction of what I could be doing. I imagined all the emotions that I am not suffering, all the sights, sounds and feeling that I am not experiencing. I could weep at the limitations which I have let myself fall into. What am I doing here? What effect am I having on this Himalayan Paradise and what effect is it having on me? We have nothing to do with each other. I am in the worst sense of the word a tourist. A dilettante picking at things that do not concern me and are not concerned with me. But you're very young, they say. The experience will be good for you, broaden your mind. For what? I say. I have a conscience about being idle. About living as a man of leisure. I would like to carry as much as a porter does, but I'm pathetically unable to – both for physical and social reasons. They belong here, I do not. I'm sure they laugh at us incongruous white-skinned feebletons!

Half an hour ago I was content. We have had a little bit of everything, relaxation, effort, heat, cold, mirth and strife. Nothing in excess. But then the meeting of the two groups. What have they been doing, what have we been doing? Why is Rudolf a casualty? Because he saw that we were wasting our time? You can't be wasting your time if you're experiencing something NEW! *What new? We are hidebound by our own English pettiness. Even the Americans saw through it and pulled out. We take our own little world of Marmite and Vesta curry and live in a little capsule wherever we go. The capsule of the Land Rover, the capsule of the Maréchal tent. When do we ever get to grips with the people, the rock, the stones? We insulate ourselves with huge Hawkins climbing boots. What are we? Floating scum.*

I despise them all except Q. He has problems of his own which he visibly fights. You can see the struggle of humanity within him. But the others. God! Weak, self-satisfied, indulgent, cooing and billing while there's a war on. S. unable to shake off his heritage of benevolent pongoism. Imagine how it rankles, seeing it in someone even younger than me.

But worst of all I despise myself. I want to get out of this cosseted existence. It's ruining me. There's work to be done. Millions to feed, although that's a hackneyed argument. Every moment the wine-press is screwing harder into the skull, until it crushes it. It's ruining Jen.

While he wrote, Thomas was aware of a beggar woman. An old hag stood three feet from his writing hand. The thoughts came to him and he wrote them down hurriedly. He winced at the soft words of the beggar woman.

"Sahb, sahb." She interrupted his thoughts. He flicked over a page, looked up at her in anger and continued writing. "Sahb?"

"Bugger off!" The woman was patient. Thomas stopped writing and looked at her. He considered her without shyness; he gazed fearlessly into her eyes.

"Who do you think I am, bloody Jesus Christ? They don't make us like that any more you know."

"Sahb?"

"You are no longer a white man's burden. I disown you." Thomas stuffed his diary into his haversack. He swung the haversack onto his shoulder and continued up the path. He was conscious of the eyes of the beggar woman. They found his spine, either with a sigh or with a curse.

"We've been waiting for you," said Simon. He and Quintin materialised at a porter's rest.

"You needn't have bothered," said Thomas. "I would have caught you up soon enough."

"Well don't mind us then," said Simon coldly.

"Don't let us hold you back, Hercules," added Quintin.

"Don't worry, I won't." Thomas marched on. He wanted to be alone. "Couple of pansies!" he muttered to himself.

"You'd have thought he might have said hello," said Simon, "and thank you for waiting."

"Stopped to pass the time of day," added Quintin. "But no, on she goes."

"Inconsiderate as you please."

"Without so much as a by your leave. I could slap his wrists."

Thomas turned round:

"Bloody queers!" he roared and went on walking.

Rick and Val sat on a rock.

"It's that bloody bird again," said Rick. "Four pointless notes. I can't get them out of my head. You can't tell where they're coming from. They seem to echo everywhere."

"It's better than the screeching one. That has me on the verge of hysterics." Val lay back on the rock. The sun was warm. She had no shirt on: her breasts spread milkily in the sunlight. Rick said:

"I wish we had a few more days."

"We do."

"I mean just me and you."

"You think too much." Rick stroked her ribs.

"Hey, you're keeping the sun off." Rick lay back on the rock. He sniffed under his armpits; they smelled of curry.

"Hey, do your armpits smell of curry?" He sniffed Val's armpit. "Yes they do!"

"God, how disgusting," said Val lazily.

"It must get carried through the sweat glands. We've had so much of it our pores are literally oozing with the stuff."

"I've got chillies growing out of my ears."

"Where?" Rick chewed Val's ear.

Thomas crashed through the bamboo. He saw Rick and Val on the rock, naked to the waist.

"Sodom and Gomorrah!" he said.

"Oh, Thomas." Rick propped himself up on his elbow. "We thought you were miles ahead."

"Well I'm not." Thomas looked at Rick and away again, but could not keep his eyes from Val's milky breasts.

"This trip seems to have turned into an orgy of one sort or another."

"Oh does it?" Rick sat up. He saw only the outline of Thomas, and the high crown of his head against the glare of the sun.

"I would have thought, you know, English people would have -."

"Would have what?" Rick played with the chain around his neck.

"- had more sense of decorum," said Thomas.

"Oh." Rick did not want to argue.

"It would be alright if she had a decent pair of breasts."

"She what?"

"But she hasn't, she's almost completely flat-chested." Val sat up.

"Oo, the sauce of it!" she said. Thomas retreated a little.

"What's wrong with those? They're perfectly ordinary breasts." She cupped her hands underneath them.

"She's like a man."

"Mighty strange man, that's all I can say," protested Val.

"Say Thomas, are you alright?" asked Rick.

"No I'm not! And neither are you. The whole of this group's gone to pot. If it's not you and Val it's Simon and Quintin pooving about."

"I think he feels left out of it," said Val. "Hey darling, come here."

"No." Thomas hesitated. "I disapprove of loose women." He turned and walked up the path.

"He *is* mixed up," said Val.

"I can understand it though," said Rick.

"Even about my breasts?"

"Now that," said Rick, "I cannot understand." He bent down to suck one of her breasts.

POKHARA, NEPAL

IN THE VILLAGE STREET, men sat in the doorways and did nothing: thin Caucasians with long faces, and angular backs of the head. Thomas smelled human faeces, the permanent smell of habitation wherever there was no frost at night. The man driving his cattle stopped to look at Thomas. He was a gangly and vulnerable, thin-legged man. He had never carried a porter's load. Thomas wanted to kick him out of the way.

A lorry carrying stone whirred from a quarry. It lurched on the uneven stones of the track, spewing diesel fumes and dust. Thomas stopped breathing as it passed. The crash of metal was a new noise. The grinning faces of the driver and his mate were the faces of enemies. They were the faces of Mogul conquerors. Thomas walked into Pokhara. The metal huts of the British Mission Hospital were on his left. Why did they do it? he asked himself. Why did they involve themselves in this mess, and accelerate its growth? The town enveloped him. It was like a chamber of horrors. But the greatest horror was the impermanence. He could not believe that the people and their wooden buildings would be there tomorrow. Or if they survived the day, what about the monsoon, or an epidemic? It was a grotesque pageant to the transience of human life. Thomas offered to his god the most urgent of prayers: "Oh Lord, let me not be like one of these." He came through the horrors alive and found himself at the airport.

KATHMANDU, NEPAL

"Great Scott! It's Captain Oates!" Rick strode forward to shake Rudolf by the hand. Rudolf reclined in an armchair, one leg resting on a stool, in the bar of the Crystal Hotel. The ankle was heavily bandaged. "Have you broken it?" asked Rick.

"No. It's a rather severe sprain. I had to be carried for four hours on the back of a porter. Absolute agony. However, that's beside the point. Pull up a chair."

"Glad to see you've fallen on your other foot at the Crystal anyway."

"Very funny. The reason I've summoned you here today is quite simple. I thought it right to let you know that I shall be taking legal proceedings against your company."

"And why's that?"

"I should have thought it was obvious. Negligence in the field. Irresponsibility on the part of the expedition leader. Lack of adequate medical supplies *and* knowledge. If it weren't for Jen I probably wouldn't be alive to tell the tale. You've no idea how serious my condition had become by the time I got back to civilisation. Lack of concern generally for the health and well-being of paying clients. Lack of information about the terrain and conditions of the trek. If I'd known what it was going to be like I would never have embarked on such an ill-considered enterprise. Forced to sleep in caves, to endure wet and cold. I'm as tough as the next man, but when one has been ill for some time, and one's resistance is down, it's foolish to continue. Craig should have seen that. Craig should have been able to sacrifice the glory of disappearing under an avalanche in favour of the general safety of the expedition. I've said it before and I'll say it again, this company of yours does not know how to behave. It's running risks which no sane person would dare to contemplate. It shoulders irresponsible people (and I don't mean this personally) with too much responsibility. And the time has come when it must be held to account. I shall make sure that it pays for it. Lord knows, my action may prevent even worse catastrophes befalling innocent punters." Rick scratched his head.

"I can't help feeling you're exaggerating the whole thing somewhat."

"If anything I'm playing it down. It's not little jaunts round the park we're dealing with. It's human lives and safety - the lives of British citizens. One can easily be blasé about these things until the worst happens, and then it's usually too late. Believe me, I'm not the sort of person to make trouble without feeling sure that he's justified. But the moment, Rick, has come."

"You don't think that your view is slightly coloured by you own personal experiences? Not everyone has had as rough a time of it as you did. Some of them have actually enjoyed it."

"They were lucky. You see there again your company relies entirely on the role of chance. If the majority of people get enough out of it, or if they are easy-going and weak-minded enough to be persuaded that they're enjoying themselves, then hey presto! The firm wins every time. But what they haven't reckoned with is someone like me, sticky enough not to be hoodwinked into thinking he's having the time of his life, and perceptive enough to realise that it is they and not I who are falling down on their duty."

"I doubt very much whether you'll be able to argue that within the terms of the contract. These travel companies cover themselves pretty carefully, you know."

"Of course they do! But that doesn't protect them from the sort of exposure that I intend to give this fiasco. Newspapers can be pretty damaging organs wielded in the right way."

"I see. Well, it's not really any concern of mine. I'm only an employee of the company. In fact I'm not even that, yet. Craig might have something a bit more concrete to say when he gets back."

"I'm sure he will. All the same, I thought I'd let you know what my intentions are."

"Thank you."

"And by the way."

"Yes?"

"Not a word of this to the others. I don't want to spoil their holiday."

"I say, that's awfully sporting of you."

"Aren't you going to buy yourself a drink?"

"No, I think I'll be getting back thanks very much. Goodbye. Get that leg working soon." Rick left the bar. He took the lift to the ground floor. He couldn't suppress a chuckle.

Marshall sorted camera films on his unmade bed.

"It was the lack of oxygen that defeated us," he told Rick. Conrad lay on his bed reading a book. "Above ten thousand feet," continued Marshall, "the condition of the body will always deteriorate. Protein levels, sugar levels, etcetera cannot be restored at that altitude, no matter how much you eat. We needed oxygen, we found our energies leaving us, and disappointing though it was we were forced to return to habitable levels."

"Some people have gotten to twenty-eight thousand feet without oxygen," said Conrad, not looking up from his book.

"They were nuts," shouted Marshall. "They will have sustained irreparable brain damage. The US Air Force advises its pilots to connect oxygen supplies after ten thousand feet."

Rick looked at the state of the room. He saw loose clothes on the floor and under the bed. Sleeping bags, rope and rucksacks were heaped in a corner. A towel lay under the wash-basin.

"It may be something to do with acclimatisation," said Rick. "If you have weeks to get used to it then -."

"In the end you will find yourself run down, irritable, unable to make valid judgments and decisions. Altitude sickness displays all the symptoms of severe exhaustion, but the condition may be chronic. In short you are liable to finish up a nut-case."

"Some of us don't have to go all that way to end up the same," said Conrad, still staring into his book.

"In that case," said Rick, "Thomas and I must be on the verge of lunacy. We went up to nearly seventeen thousand feet."

"Without oxygen?" queried Marshall.

"And you're driving us back to England?" said Conrad. "God preserve us." Rick smiled at Conrad.

"When did you get back from Everest?"

"About a week back," said Conrad. "We had a great time. Really wild. We weren't allowed to go above ten thousand feet. Every drop of water we drank we boiled for ten minutes. No beer. No talking after eight o'clock. We see a few green valleys that you can see any place. Then we fly back. It was great."

"Did you do much walking?"

"Oh, yuh. Down to the airstrip to find if we could get the next plane home."

"Sounds fun. Are you coming to eat? My lot's having lunch at the Nook today."

"Sure," said Conrad. He sprang from the bed. "Marshall?" he asked.

"Thanks. I have some work to do. I may join you later."

Dear Ignatius,

We have learned a good deal on our trek in Nepal about the limitations of human endurance, and the limitations of the human mind. Few problems arose that we did not anticipate. We were well equipped, but what we attempted to do, we achieved without oxygen.

Oxygen was not available in Lukla, contrary to what we had been led to believe. So our ceiling, in keeping with Air Force regulations, did not exceed ten thousand feet. The physique of my companion hardly encouraged the taking of risks at greater altitude, much as I would have been prepared to run them on my own.

There are many Japanese around Everest. They are building a hotel with a spectacular view. Oxygen is supplied to each room. There is a road extending to the Tibetan border, built by the Chinese. Anglo-Saxons are not allowed to use it. Chinese infiltration of Nepal continues. We saw goods and advisers from over the border.

Kathmandu however is a capital with a healthily Western flavor. The hamburgers are superb. Dollars fetch a good price on the black market. Investigations of my own concerning the legal sale of hashish, and the type of Westerners who come here solely for the purpose of using it, have led me to believe -.

. . .

Marshall put down his pen. From the pocket of his anorak he took a package of silver paper. He unwrapped the package and exposed a lump of brown resin. He laid it on the table. From another pocket he drew out tobacco, matches, and cigarette paper. He broke a piece from the lump of resin. He struck a match and heated the resin, kneading it until it was soft. In his hands he mixed it with the tobacco. He rolled the mixture in a cigarette paper, put the tube to his lips and lit it. As he inhaled he closed his eyes. Marshall picked up his pen and continued:

- that the main offenders are regrettably to be found among our own countrymen. With my own eyes I have seen kids from the Mid-West begging in the streets like natives. All they want is a handful of rupees to buy their next ticket to oblivion, a few ounces of pot. Who can say that they are not already becoming enslaved by some more damnable drug? The civilised intellect revolts at the thought of such tampering with its processes. It is a habit which attacks the entire Western culture at its roots. It absolves one of the desire to struggle and improve one's lot. What could be more dangerous in the sphere of un-American activities?

Marshall rose to his feet. He floated to his bed and lay down, scattering the canisters of film. The window frame contained a delicate painting. Sunlight was captured perfectly on the telegraph pole, the concrete wall. A fluffy cloud, bottom-heavy with rain, seemed almost to move across the canvas.

"Pure Gainsborough," he murmured. From landscape into portrait, the foreground became a head, hideous and swollen. A mouth grinned at Marshall, painted lips and a quartered golfing cap. Marshall sat up to observe the phenomenon more closely.

"Sherpa," he told himself. The door opened. The detached head floated into the room.

"They tell me you've gone barmy," it said. "Altitude sickness."

"That's right," Marshall leaned back. "It's a real gas."

"You've been smoking hash." Steve took off his golfing cap and waved it in the air. "Christ!" Marshall offered him the half-smoked joint. Steve accepted it, took a puff, and trod it into the floor.

"Now wait a minute!" Marshall looked at the cigarette on the floor. "What did you do that for?"

Steve blew smoke from his mouth. "Because it's not your scene, man." He turned and examined the state of the room. "This place is a mess, Marshall, it needs cleaning up." Steve paced up and down, his hands behind his back. Marshall watched him without protest.

"Who sent you along?" he asked. Steve smiled and replaced his golfing cap.

"The FBI," he said. "So watchit." He left the room.

Marshall went to sleep. When he woke up it was getting dark. Conrad had come in, changed, and gone out again.

"I'm hungry," said Marshall. He swung himself from his bed. Film canisters clattered to the floor. He put on his anorak and walked to the Nook.

"Thomas was rather wearing," said Val.

"He's very young," Jen countered. "And because he's not sure of himself he tends to be aggressive."

"Downright belligerent at times," said Val. "D'you know what he called me? 'A loose woman', 'concubine,' 'we all heard you and Rick at it, it's absolutely disgusting'. Things like that."

"So you've moved on to Rick, have you?"

"He's very sweet and he's absolutely crazy about me, which helps."

"And what about Craig?"

"I haven't seen him yet. He's such a bastard. Did he talk much about me?"

"Not a word, darling."

"I suppose he started making up to you."

"Hardly. He was very nice to Win though."

"Oh?"

"In a joking sort of way. You see it was only four of us. Rather cosy really. We had a good time of it in the end. Although at the beginning I was almost in despair."

"I must say Win looks very fit now, like a satisfied porker."

"Oh it was nothing like that. We just got to know each other very well, that's all. Win's got an awful lot to her."

"Has she. And what about your Steve? How did he behave?"

"He was completely different in the mountains. So strong and gentle. I wish we could always be in the mountains."

"So the frog turned into the fairy prince. Is that why Rudolf left?"

"Rudolf was ill, very ill."

"Psychosomatic?"

"Maybe. But he wasn't faking – he really looked ill. And now he seems to have sprained his ankle. He is an old misery. You should have seen him. 'I feel as weak as a baby,' he said. I had to wipe his mouth with a hanky. He said he was sick with love for me."

"I knew it."

"No. He was just saying that because he needed sympathy. And the next morning he left. We were quite worried about him."

"I'm sure he got satisfaction out of that."

"I pity the poor little man who had to carry him on his back. 'We don't want to spend our last seconds falling over a cliff now do we, *nota bene*'. 'Aye aye sahib.' He's invited me to dinner at the Crystal Hotel 'in recognition of my services to medicine.'"

"Are you going?"

"It seems so silly. But I suppose I'll have to."

"If Steve will let you."

"Oh, he couldn't care less. He's back to his old self. He says I can marry Rudolf if I like – all he wants is his bit on the side."

"Cool bugger."

"How about little Simon?"

"What about him? Oh, I think he and Quintin agreed to disagree, if you see what I mean."

"Poor Quintin, it seems such a waste."

"How do you mean, a waste?"

"Such a nice, intelligent man infatuated with a boy who happens to be straight."

"How do you know he's straight? He did go to public school, didn't he? He might be bit of both."

"But they're not all like that. Rudolf is not like that."

"How do you know? He's pretty odd, isn't he. I would have thought he could swing either way."

"Poor Simon."

"Poor us."

Rudolf leaned on his crutch at the bar. "But dash it, why hasn't he come to see me himself?" He glowered at Rick.

"He says he's busy. He says if you want to sue, sue away."

"I shall. My case is getting stronger every day."

"In the meantime Craig wonders whether you will be honouring us with your presence on the return trip, or whether, as you hinted, you have other plans."

"Other plans," said Rudolf. He finished his gin. "I shall be flying to Delhi, and on to Srinagar. You'll be picking me up in Srinagar."

"That sounds a good move. Give you a bit of a rest from the mob anyway. Driving through India isn't much fun."

"My main motive is to rest this little lot." Rudolf slapped his leg. "But of course there are other reasons. Ah, Jennifer, lovely to see you." Jen arrived through the door. "Alright Rick, that will be all. Report to your master."

"Cheeky bugger," said Rick to himself as he left the bar. Jen stood three feet from Rudolf and smiled. She was wearing a skirt.

"How's the invalid?" she said.

"All the better for seeing you. You look absolutely ripping. What are you having to drink?"

"Campari and soda, if they've got it."

"Good gel! Well, we meet in rather pleasanter circumstances than when we last saw each other. Campari and soda and another gin. We can go and sit down."

"Is your leg very painful?"

"Bearing up, bearing up." Rudolf eased himself into a chair. "I'm very grateful to you. For looking after me in those beastly mountains."

"I didn't look after you. I was rather horrid to you."

"That's the best treatment. The best medicine you can give someone like me."

"But one of us should have stayed with you. I'm sure of that now."

"That wasn't for you to decide, was it. You weren't supposed, unlike someone else we know, to be leading an expedition. If he falls down on the job, are you to blame? Not a bit. You behaved admirably."

"Anyway I'm glad to see you're safe and sound."

"By the skin of my teeth I can assure you."

"Are you coming back with us or are you going to fly?"

"Now that will be one of the talking points of the evening." Rudolf chuckled. "We'll come back to that one." The bearer brought a gin and a Campari on a tray, together with a soda syphon. Jen spilt soda on the table. They went in to dinner. The meal progressed.

"I've always hoped to have one evening like this with you," said Rudolf. "So that we could really get to know something about each other. Those Land Rovers are all very well, but they hardly encourage decent conversation between two people. One has to be able to live in public as it were. Now Steve, there you are, you see, does it very well. He regards all his thoughts and his likes and dislikes as public property. And so he lives like a kind of tribune of the people. You've fallen for it, we all have. But I'm not like that myself, I prefer to keep my thoughts bottled up inside, unless -."

"Unless what?"

"Unless there is someone to whom I particularly want to divulge them."

"I suppose you mean me."

"Right." Rudolf paused, knife and fork in hand. A lump of meat glistened on the fork. Jen, who had finished her steak, watched in fascination as it disappeared into Rudolf's mouth.

She ordered fruit trifle to follow and ate it with relish.

"I'm enjoying this evening immensely," she said. Rudolf, elbows on the table, hands clasped under his chin replied:

"I'm glad. Coffee? Liqueur?"

"Both, I'm afraid."

"You know it's a pleasure to see you tucking in like that. Healthy appetite and so on. I suppose you're a bit of a country girl at home."

"I adore the country. I can't live without it. You know I had a job in London once, with an advertising agency. I couldn't stand more than a month of it, it was so claustrophobic. So I went back home and worked for our MP."

"Conservative of course."

"I'm afraid so."

"Now why are you afraid? Because you think it's fashionable to be left wing? Because you feel guilty about a class you don't belong to?"

"Please Rudolf, don't let's get into that."

"I'm sorry. I nearly spoiled a wonderful evening. But Jen," he put his hand on hers, "don't be afraid of what you are." Jen looked at Rudolf and withdrew her hand.

"What do you think I am?"

"I won't tell you what I think. Here comes our coffee. Shall we have it in the lounge?" Jen helped Rudolf to walk to the lounge. The bearer followed with the coffee.

"I must say I've seen a completely different side of you this evening," she said.

"Have you now? It's been there all the time you know, it just needed a little encouragement."

"I didn't want to encourage it too far."

"What do you mean?" Jen looked at Rudolf and laughed.

"Oh, I don't know."

"Tell me about your childhood."

"Very boring. Tell me about yours." Jen gulped her liqueur.

"Equally so. I'm not a rakish vicar's son, nor an infant prodigy. I've never been particularly good at anything as you may have noticed." Rudolf glanced at his bandages.

"I don't see how being good at things has any bearing on real life, though."

"But it's what we're brought up to believe in, all the same. Excellence at all sports and disciplines."

"That sort of thing went out years ago. It's what you are that matters. Whether you're a good person."

"That's even worse. Going round judging whether we've been good or not. I wouldn't stand a chance. On the other hand -." Rudolf looked at Jen. "I could mention someone who rates pretty highly on several scales."

"Oh?"

"Barring one terrible vice."

"Doesn't sound like anyone I know. Tell me about the vice, though. I love hearing about vices."

"No, no, I couldn't possibly in front of a lady." Rudolf took a cigar out of his inside pocket. "I won't offer you one," he said.

"How disappointing." Rudolf removed the label. He took out a cutter and clipped the end. He took out a box of matches and lit the cigar.

"I didn't know you smoked," said Jen.

"Cigars are different." Rudolf leaned back in his chair. He blew smoke into the air. "Now Jen I'll tell you what I plan to do."

"Is this the great talking point of the evening coming up?"

"Yes. I shall be flying to Delhi sometime this week. After a few days there, seeing a few people, that sort of thing, I shall fly on to Srinagar. Craig should arrive there in approximately ten days' time, which means there'll be no hurry. I can relax and enjoy myself."

"Sounds ideal."

"Do you know Srinagar? By all reports it's the most divine place: the Venice of the East. And instead of the heat of India it'll be winter there, snow on the mountains, ice on the lakes. Apparently you can stay on a little houseboat, warm as toast, just like an English cottage in the middle of the lake."

"How absolutely charming. Are you sure you're not making it up? It sounds too good to be true."

"I have it on the best authority. I think it will do me, it would do anyone, a power of good, just a few days of real relaxation."

"I do envy you. I don't have the money to do that sort of thing. Flying here, having a night in a decent hotel there. I'm sure that's the way one ought to travel. It gives you more time and energy to look about you."

"Exactly. I've had enough of Land Rovers. To say nothing of the people inside them."

"Yes, I suppose we are a bit of an ordeal."

"Not you," said Rudolf. "They."

"I'm just as bad." Rudolf was silent. He puffed his cigar.

"More Cointreau?"

"I ought to be going." Rudolf looked at his watch.

"Good lord! Yes, I suppose you ought."

"It's been a lovely evening. I'm very glad you asked me to come. I've thoroughly enjoyed myself as well as eating like a pig."

"I must say I found it tolerably entertaining myself. I'll order a taxi. Please excuse me for not being in a fit state to see you home."

"Oh, don't bother to get up."

"Nonsense. Besides," said Rudolf, as he hobbled with her to the door. "I haven't finished yet." He ordered a taxi. At the entrance to the hotel he spoke again. "Now Jen, with reference to my aeronautics on the sub-continent of India, I'd like you to travel with me as my guest."

"But Rudolf!"

"Don't squeak about it. Have a think. Sleep on it. Give me your answer in the morning. Goodnight, god bless." Rudolf turned on his crutch and limped into the hotel.

"Ridiculous!" said Jen. She looked after Rudolf. The taxi driver waited for her to climb in. "Rudolf," she murmured.

. . .

Sun played on the one peak visible from the Withies Hotel. Dew left the chairs and tables on the lawn. Mr Withy, immaculate in his turban, brought a breakfast tray into the sunlight. Craig poured himself a cup of tea. Val sat opposite him, one leg crossed over the other. Her eyes were half-closed in the glare.

"Aren't you going to pour me one?" she said.

"Help yourself." Craig bit into a slice of soggy toast. Val smiled. She poured herself a cup.

The Land Rover stood ten yards away, clean and unladen. Rick worked on one of the wheels. A jack supported the front axle. The tyre lay near him on its side. He took a series of tools from the tool-box, like a surgeon, and exposed the hub. He did not whistle.

"What are you making him do this time?" asked Val. Craig looked at her. He wondered whether it was worth saying.

"Oil seal," he said.

"Is that very serious?"

"Prophylaxis." Val didn't understand.

"You're a bastard," she said.

"I didn't think you cared."

"One has to live with you, you know, for another six weeks at any rate."

"You don't have to stay. You can play hard-to-get like Rudolf."

"He's asked Jen to go with him. Did you know that?"

"Fairly obvious."

"She might be going. You didn't expect that, did you?"

"I don't know. Birds of a feather."

"She was in hysterics with Steve this morning. I'd hate them to split up. Especially for the sake of that Rudolf creature."

"I don't suppose she'll do anything you don't want her to."

"Why do you say that?"

"Because I believe it." Val tried to read Craig's expression. She glanced at Rick and sighed.

"You men are impossible. I'll have to go and speak to Jen." She walked into the hotel. Craig drank his cup of tea. He walked to the Land Rover and crouched beside Rick.

"How is it?"

"Bloody terrible. I can't get this collar off."

"Oh, I shouldn't bother about the collar." Rick stopped chiselling.

"Well, it's too late now," he said. "I've chiselled half-way through it."

"Here." Craig picked up the hammer and chisel. "You find you have to hit it pretty hard. Sod!" He sucked his bruised thumb. He hammered again. "There we are. Now we've got to put the new one on."

"I'll do it," said Rick.

"OK." Craig stood up. He sucked his thumbnail. Jen came out of the hotel. She smiled.

"Hello Craig." Her eyes were not red. But she walked quickly to the gate and along the road into town.

"Was that Jen?" asked Rick. "She was making a noise and a half this morning. Not like her usual self."

"One of the many crises of identity."

"What's she going to do, do you think?"

"Saw herself in half." Craig mused with his hands in his pockets. "Here!" he yelled. The boy with the tray in his hands put it back on the table. "Little monkey." He walked to the table and poured himself another cup of tea. Thomas came out of the hotel to talk to him.

"Craig, what about packing up the Land Rover?"

"It should be done by twelve."

"Aren't you going to tell people to do it? They're just lazing about in there."

"They'll do it," said Craig.

"I see," said Thomas. He played with the back of the chair. "Well -" he said. He walked to the Land Rover and stood by Rick. "Having trouble?"

"Yup."

Marshall and Conrad arrived by taxi. Marshall argued with the taxi driver.

"Eight rupees! That's a helluva lot to pay for a mile ride. I don't have eight rupees." He dropped a bundle of notes to the ground.

"Guess who's back," said Thomas. He was pleased to see new faces. He walked towards Marshall and Conrad. They carried their kitbags, ropes and rucksacks. Conrad trailed his ice-axe.

"My god, no wonder you only made ten thousand feet," said Thomas.

"We're figuring on coming back," jibed Conrad, "to do another ten thousand. A little more each time."

By 12.15 the Land Rover was loaded. Jen had not appeared. Val and Win packed her bags and took them to the vehicle. Simon talked earnestly with Conrad. Quintin smoked at one of the tables. Steve did not talk. He kicked at stones. No one ventured to speak to him. Val spoke with Craig.

"We'll drive down to the Crystal," said Craig. "Then everyone can have lunch. It's near all the restaurants." Craig parked in the main street.

"They do an excellent wild boar at the Paras," said Thomas.

"We're going to the Indira. It's a bit more civilised," said Simon.

"A trifle more," said Quintin, "and oh for one more trifle."

Steve followed Rick to the Capital for a last buffalo steak and crisps.

"Of course Marshall and Conrad have scuttled off to the Nook," jeered Thomas. "Win, won't you come and have a wild boar with me?" She smiled:

"Alright." Val and Craig entered the Crystal Hotel. They inquired for Rudolf's room. The lift took them to the third floor.

"Come in," said Rudolf. Jen lay on the bed. Rudolf sat in a wicker chair.

"Hullo," said Jen.

"Do you realise what time it is?" exploded Val.

"We're having a soul-search," said Jen.

"No time for lost souls, I'm afraid," said Val. "We're leaving in an hour."

"Are you?" said Jen vaguely.

"And we think you'd better come along too," said Val. Jen raised herself and looked at them.

"Have you made it up then, you and Craig?"

"No, we're deadly enemies," said Craig. "But we need you to keep the peace."

"Oh dear." Jen blew her nose.

"Now look here." Rudolf raised himself on his crutch. "I don't know what your game is, but I think Jen should be allowed to decide for herself. I've made her an offer, and only she knows what she'd prefer to do. The rest of us must keep out of it."

"But Steve is waiting for you, Jen. He wants you," said Val.

"He doesn't want me. He'd be here if he wanted me."

"That's not his way. You know that as well as I do. But he wants you alright. You both want each other. You're like a pair of children."

"Jen's a mature woman. She's quite capable of determining her own future. And she's coming with me."

"No she's not!" shouted Val. "You're an old-fashioned prig.

You're a puritan bigot, you're a chinless, mindless twit. Anyone can see that."

"I'm a what?!"

"You think, because you've got more money than anyone else you can buy yourself out of living with people. But you can't buy other people out as well. Jen doesn't want to share your absurd Edwardian world with you, however much you may seduce her with dinners and air tickets and houseboats in Kashmir. Jen wants a man, not a wimp with a moustache, and a pretty pathetic one at that. Come on Jen." Val took Jen by the hand and dragged her out of the room. Jen held her hand over her mouth.

"Oh god, what have I done?" she sobbed loudly. Craig stood in the doorway.

"We'll see you in Srinagar in about nine days then. Goodbye." He closed the door behind him.

Thomas wrote in his diary:

We left Kathmandu at half-past one, without Rudolf. Jen was very subdued, and not talking to Steve. We spent the night camping at the Daman Pass. Most of the mountains were covered in cloud, but as we left in the morning we saw milky outlines just shining through, way up in the sky. It's exhausting and irritating being back in the Land Rover, but it's not as bad as I dreaded. We even sang songs. Home in six weeks!

GANDAK RIVER, INDIA

From Raxaul on the border of Nepal it was impossible to drive west to Delhi. The Gandak river, the same that ran down from Tibet through the Himalayas, plunged into India and flowed south to join the Ganges. There was no bridge across it. The main road kept east of the Gandak and only when it has crossed the Ganges below Patna could it turn west.

But there was another way. Craig wanted to find the legendary ferry which took vehicles across the Gandak, from Govindganj on one side, to Gopalganj on the other.

Govindganj didn't seem to exist. The road gave way to a dusty track. A collection of huts might have had a name, but they didn't constitute a place. Craig took the track southward. The road was waterlogged in places. For a second they had a glimpse of the broad river. There were dykes, defences against the monsoon. A few lights from fires shone on the flat cultivated plain. But the travellers were lost. Darkness descended quickly and they made camp.

A light breeze, almost a sea-breeze, blew over the dykes, but the river was not to be seen. Tom-toms sounded from a nearby village. Villagers on their way home from the fields paused to look at the encampment. Thirty Indians stood at a respectful distance, murmuring among themselves.

"Govindganj?" asked Craig. "Feribotrod?" The Indians conferred together. For the first time the travellers were faced with Indians who could not speak English – not a word among them.

They murmured. They watched the Europeans go to bed. When the white men seemed asleep they drifted away in twos and tens. The tom-toms continued. Until midnight the odd villager with his cart passed on the sandy road.

Towards three, when all was quiet, thunder sounded from the Himalayas. It shocked the walls of thick air, but from a safe distance. At four o'clock a thunderclap announced that the storm had advanced. The travellers felt no rain. They refused to see consequences in the black bank of cloud from the north. It towered vertically above them, but for a while no rain fell.

Then fat drops began to explode around them. A wind tugged across the tree plantation. It became strong and less playful. The tarpaulin on the roof-rack smacked against itself. Rain came as a relief, hard and positive, kicking up spurts of dust.

Eleven people dived into the Land Rover together with their bedding. Water hammered on metal. Lightning froze the night in brilliance. Thunder crashed onto the lightning, punishing it and spending itself along the bellies of the clouds. The drama continued for three minutes. The avenging angel had passed overhead. The rain stopped. A sound of breathing filled the vehicle.

As it grew light the trees were swaying no more. The ground was bone dry. The tourists opened the aluminium doors and stretched their legs. They pulled their faces back into shape. They drove on south along a bullock track with its undulating ruts of dust, odd puddles and mud pans. The road led past primitive huts to more fields beyond. They met a bus. The driver encouraged them to continue south. Craig was beginning to lose confidence.

"Are you sure this ferry exists?" asked Marshall.

"Sure," said Craig. Just then they hit a tarmac road running west. After a mile, there was the Gandak river, broad and flat. The road led to a ramp which appeared to span the river but it ended abruptly: the bridge had not yet been built. Pontoons defined its future course across the current to a ramp on the other side. There were two landing craft moored there. Through his binoculars Marshall could see washing hanging on the deck, but no sign of life. Craig gave a blast on the horn. Some workers on one of the pontoons looked up.

"We might as well brew some tea," said Craig. So they collected driftwood and lit a fire. The sun rose behind them though it was not yet hot.

Thomas spotted what looked like a coracle in mid-stream with two men punting it. A jeep arrived along a sandy track. The driver got out – a dark face behind sunglasses.

"Is there a ferry?" asked Craig. The driver pointed to the coracle.

"This is ferry."

"That thing?" Craig borrowed Marshall's binoculars. "I suppose it might take us one at a time."

"No," said the driver, "this jeep, that jeep, traili, all going on."

The travellers drank tea. The confidence of this man in sunglasses seemed misplaced. The craft was just too small. It looked as though they had a long drive south to Patna.

The coracle heaved itself onto the muddy shore. It was a patchwork construction of bamboo and earth. Planks were lowered into the water. The jeep, submerged to the axles, charged up the planks and onto the deck, its front wheels stopping inches from the far edge.

One of the ragged coracle men took Craig by the sleeve and showed him the craft. The sheer amount of bamboo, reinforced with grass and mud, looked more solid than he had expected. If the trailer were crammed at the bow the Land Rover could just about hang itself amidships, he thought, with its bumpers over the water each side.

Ten men appeared from nowhere and helped to waltz the trailer onto its bamboo bed. The planks were shifted to the middle. Craig, alone at the wheel, selected the lowest gear and charged up the planks. The vehicle, beast-like, heaved itself onto the deck, to a loud cheer.

Then the coracle, which was now stuck in the mud, was rocked and pushed by helping hands. The quanting poles were ready for action, but the crew would not start until both drivers had paid an inflated fare. As the coracle swung into the current some of the other passengers took up their instruments, a trumpet, a French horn, a pipe and a drum and began to play.

"Wedding," said the jeep driver.

On the other side the procedure was reversed and the Land Rover and trailer were soon on dry land. The only casualty, left on the far shore, was a white jerry can.

DELHI, INDIA

Quintin was on his hotel bed writing a letter:

Dear Toby,
I feel like a starving man before the most sumptuous feast spread out on a table, knowing that I cannot, no I may not, touch a morsel. To do so would be to jeopardise everything, even the small comfort of being able to dream about gorging myself on this forbidden fruit. You know of what I speak.

The horror of it is, in ten days, less, he will be gone. I can think of nothing to cheer myself. Even committing this sad tale to paper does me no good at all. I want, and I cannot have. Somewhere it has been written.

That apart, a flirtation with death on Charon's ferry, two foot by four foot, and a day of roads too cruel for the snake on his exile from Eden. We are now in Delhi.

Christmas has stolen up on us. Connaught Circus is arrayed with coloured light-bulbs. Rich Indians strut about in their tight trousers and pointed shoes. Film stars take coffee in the open

restaurants: the fountains play. We don't know how to celebrate this festive season. The easiest way is to get drunk.
God bless,
Q.

The United Coffee House offered a three-course Christmas luncheon. They had agreed to eat there. Craig entered at two o'clock. He scanned the ground floor; there were no English to be seen. He climbed the stairs. In the gallery three tables were joined together seating twenty people.

"Craig!" A shout rose above the din.

"Jerry!" Jerry - last seen when his and Craig's Land Rovers crossed paths in eastern Turkey - stretched out his arms. His new charges sat about him, large and small, old and young.

"This is Veronica," he said. His hand rested on the shoulder of a small girl, dark, with thick lips. "We call her Wonks." The other members laughed quietly. Craig's group sat at one end of the complex. They talked among themselves. "I've met your lot before, haven't I," said Jerry. "We've had a bloody cold trip, but they're a great crowd, aren't they Wonks?"

"When did you leave?"

"Late November. We bashed straight through it was so bloody cold. You've got it coming to you my boy."

"I like the cold," said Craig.

"We kept a place for you," said Jerry. Craig sat down. He saw the face of a middle-aged woman opposite him. "That's Pat," said Jerry. "She's our hundred-year-old teenager." Pat giggled. "And this is Gordon." Gordon nodded his giant head; his shoulders towering over the heads of those next to him. "That's Murgatroid." The youth indicated peered over the table-cloth. "He's only fifteen."

"Quite a varied bunch," said Craig.

"You can say that again. It's surprising how well they get on though."

"You're an ace bullshitter."

"Now tell me where have you been to." Pat fixed Craig with twinkling, wild eyes.

"Food!" shouted Thomas from the other end of the party. The lunchers had been neglected. The tables were bare. Waiters appeared, only to rush away again.

"He sounds rather hungry," said Jerry.

"How long have you been waiting?"

"Nearly an hour. I find it quite stimulating. You don't get waits like this anywhere else in the world." A timid under-waiter stood by a sideboard stacked with condiments. He could do nothing without authorisation.

Thomas stood up. He went downstairs and scanned the squad of waiters. He selected one without a white jacket, who seemed to be in charge.

"Could you tell me," thundered Thomas, stretching to his full height of six feet two inches, "why we have not been served? We've been waiting well over an hour."

"You will be served, yes, yes. Please take a seat."

"No, 'yes, yes'!" boomed Thomas. "If we are not served within the next five minutes we'll take our custom elsewhere. We've had enough, up to here, do you understand?" Thomas turned on his heel and strode upstairs. The head waiter came to the gallery. "I told him where to get off," said Thomas. The waiter shouted through a doorway. Two more waiters appeared. The head waiter rebuked one of them, who in turn rebuked the other. More waiters were summoned. They rebuked each other in turn.

"Wait for it," said Jerry. The timid under-waiter stood by the sideboard. In a moment the full storm of abuse would hit him. There it came. Orders were barked from senior to junior.

Action began from the bottom. Knives and forks clattered in their hands. Plates and glasses rang onto the tables. Thomas folded his arms in satisfaction. Some roast turkey arrived.

"But what about our soup?" The turkey was taken away. Soup came. Chinese dishes were brought, unordered, then cold roast turkey.

"Honestly I don't care anymore, let's eat it," said Wonks. Christmas pudding followed. Pat's eyes twinkled:

"Do you have a person called Rudolf in your company? His mother asked me to write and say how he is getting on."

"Is it the first time he's left home?"

"He's such a dear boy, devoted to Marjory, his mother."

"Life and soul of the party," said Craig. "Tremendous sense of humour."

"That would be him."

"He's taken off on his own for a bit. We join him again in Kashmir."

"He likes to do things on his own."

"A natural traveller," said Craig. "Resourceful and independent."

"That's what we all try to be," said Pat. "Don't we Jerry?"

"Pat's marvellous," said Jerry. "She's our alarm clock."

"Wakes us all up with a cup of tea," said Wonks. "I don't know how she does it." Pat laughed. Thomas and Steve began to sing:

"Oh tidings of comfort and joy." The chorus followed: "Tidings of comfort and joy."

"What news from England," Craig asked Jerry.

"Business is bad. They're thinking of buying a forty-seater bus. No one wants to go on our exclusive expeditions any more."

"No one's got the money," said Gordon. His giant head nodded as he laughed.

"Are we getting any new Land Rovers?"

"No, mine's doing its fourth trip with me. I can tell you what's going to break down next."

"And what have they got lined up for me, do you know?"

"I think it's another one of these, to Everest or Kashmir, but I'm not sure."

"If I stay on."

"You will, Craig me boy. I know you better than you do yourself."

"Maybe."

"You might be fed up with it now, but a week in England and you'll be kicking and screaming to be off again. It's the same with me. We're two of a kind."

"Hah! There's only one Jerry." The group at the end of the table got up to leave.

"We're going to the Imperial," said Steve. "Come along when you're ready."

"What a bloody miserable way to spend Christmas," said Craig. Scenes of drunkenness continued. They brought drink into the rooms back at the YMCA, which was forbidden.

"Simon peed into the fountain," reported Thomas. Craig's party left the hostel on Boxing Day, in disgrace. They celebrated their exit by singing: "On the first day of Christmas." Jerry watched them leave.

SRINAGAR, INDIA

SIMON WROTE IN HIS DIARY, excited by the sudden change of scenery:

From Jammu we left the plain of India and wound up to Kashmir. The road is excellently maintained, obviously regarded as vital to the defence of Kashmir. There are military checkpoints, road tolls, and fortified bridges. As we rose higher they were still working on the road, smooth and broad enough to take tanks.

Indian summer changes into autumn. As we stopped for lunch you could smell the decay of the leaves, soft misty smells. Plenty of pine forest but the hills are more crumbling than the Alps.

At the top of the pass it is winter. We changed into boots and anoraks. A short descent into the Srinagar valley, and we drive past fields and lines of poplars just like Holland. The houses are fully, or half-timbered, slightly Elizabethan in style. It's a shock to see frost and ice, and people dressed in heavy hats and blankets. This is Muslim country again. The faces have a distinctly Persian look about them. It's difficult to imagine them as Indian.

SRINAGAR, INDIA

We arrived in Srinagar at dusk. Along the waterfront we saw the lights of many houseboats. A gangly boy in a blanket hailed a shikara and we piled in. He punted us out to a boat called Apollo Thirteen. Another gondola glided past us. It had a canopy and cushions. Of our surroundings I couldn't see much. We look forward to daylight to discover exactly where we are.

Thomas, seeing elements that would have been familiar to his favourite English writers, commented in his diary:

Apart from its name, Apollo Thirteen recalls more than anything else the inside of a country cottage in Hampshire. There are sofas and standard lamps, prints of duck-shooting on plain panelled walls, rugs and carpets on the floor. The small panes of the windows rattle. There is the enclosed sense of long winter evenings. We sit for all the world like characters in a drawing room drama waiting for the extraordinary to happen, but it never does. Jen writes in her diary. Val reads one of the many extinct paperbacks found in the bedrooms. The only un-English thing is the stove near the centre of the room, tall, austere, lending a touch of Ibsen realism, hereditary madness. Isolated we are. But then what Hampshire home of a retired colonel has evil genies tapping on the window panes? That is exactly what they look like, the smiling faces of tradesmen and hawkers who sidle up in their flat boats. They hold up necklaces and wooden carvings, silks and caskets outside in the cold.

"Mister! Silk dressing gown. All this can be yours for a very few dollars." The hooked nose scythes above the wicked smile and moustache – like a disembodied spirit it glides past the window.

This morning we could go duck shooting. We could hunt

bears in the hills. But we prefer to stay in and absorb the atmosphere of home. Is that what we travel for? To find other bits of the world that we can call home?

At eleven o'clock Thomas stood by the window in the rear of the boat, with his hands behind his back.

"Good lord, we've got a visitor," he said. A canopied punt knocked against the steps of the porch. A youth in galoshes sprang onto the deck of Apollo Thirteen and held the two boats together. A head appeared around the canopy, wearing a woollen hat with earflaps. Red nose and red rims to the eyes glowed above an icy moustache.

"Hello chaps, I thought I'd pay you a call." Rudolf swung himself onto the bigger craft. His baggage came after him. The door was opened to admit him, then closed hurriedly.

"So the prodigal has returned," said Val.

"I've brought a bottle of whisky. Perhaps we could celebrate my safe return."

"You're a godless person, Mr Rudolf, to be thinking of such a thing at this hour," said Steve. "But I'll not say no to a wee dram." Rudolf marched to the stove rubbing his hands.

"Bloody cold outside," he said.

"Tut, swearing too," said Thomas with his arms folded.

"Where are the others?"

"Minding their own business." Rudolf paused to look at Thomas. He rubbed his hands again.

"Well, we'll have some glasses," he said. "Boy!"

"Personally I shall be quite happy with tea." Thomas sat down in an armchair. He crossed one leg over the other.

"Drinking glasses," said Rudolf to the boy.

"And tea," said Thomas, "a pot of tea."

"The others have gone to look at a carpet factory," said Steve. "Except for Rick. He's in bed."

"What's wrong with him?"

"Nobody knows," said Jen. "He says he's very tired."

"Shagged out. He's been at it too much."

"Shuttup Thomas!" said Jen.

Thomas wrote in his diary:

After lunch Simon and I went punting on the lake. We followed a creek into the old part of Srinagar. It's like a complete mediaeval town built on water. Beautifully carved wooden balconies and roofs. The traffic is all by boat. Little pallets for single Muslims. They sit at the bows with their legs crossed, and paddle so that the boat looks like part of their bodies behind them, extending under a blanket. They're like sea-centaurs with little round hats. Big barges jam the streets carrying corn, firewood and sewage. The colours are monochrome as in a Dutch winter landscape. The lake is not frozen, but occasionally we broke through a skin of ice just forming. Ducks fussed out of our way. We got lost down shallow channels, but at sunset we came into the open lake. Fishermen sat in their shikaras resting like boomerangs on the water, mirrored in the dead calm. Normally we should see mountains. But over a certain altitude a bright mist obscures everything. We see lines of empty poplars – strange to find bare trees again. And the lake shines pale in the sunlight. The sun is an orange pool which no longer hurts the eyes. The sound of the ducks grows louder as the sun slips below the lake. And we punt back for tea: with bone china and buttered toast.

. . .

Jen and Steve stood by the jetty. They waited for a shikara to take them to the houseboat. The sun had set. A Muslim prayer sounded from a loud-speaker on the mosque. Lights moved on the surface of the water.

"I love you, Jen." They could not see their red eyes and noses, only white clouds of breath between them. Jen sniffed.

"You're silly. I love you too." Steve pressed his head against hers, and his body, to create pockets of warmth between them. He could not feel her shape under her clothing.

"It's difficult to face them all after being with you," said Jen. "I just want us to be alone."

"Aye lass," said Steve. He stroked her hair. A boat dipped onto the jetty.

"Sahb." A small child stepped ashore. A blanket reached his ankles. His feet rattled in shoes too big for him.

"Very cold," said Jen. The boy laughed. He drew something from under the blanket.

"Fire basket," he said. Jen put her hands over the pot and felt the warmth of the embers. The boy laughed a deep, velvet laugh.

"What is your name?" asked Jen.

"Saeed." They passed between the sterns of houseboats. They heard shouts, the emptying of buckets into water. A dog barked. "Saeed!" A voice drifted across the floating village. Saeed replied hoarsely in conversation: "Ha...ha..."

"My mother," he said. On the steps of Apollo Thirteen Jen gave him two coins. He turned to Steve.

"That's from both of us," said Steve.

"Mister, I am very cold."

"Here you are Saeed." Jen gave him a rupee note. "Meanie," she said. As they entered she held Steve by the arm.

"Tomorrow we leave for home," said Rudolf.

"But we're already on our way home, we turned round at Kathmandu," said Thomas.

"You might just as well say," cut in Simon, "that we were on our way home from the moment we left London."

"But this is the end of our holiday," said Rudolf. "There'll be no more relaxing, oh no. From tomorrow we're concerned wholly with the business of getting back to England. We've covered most of the ground before. We won't want to stop off and look at things. It'll be a rat-race to the home port."

"I think we'll enjoy seeing familiar places again," said Jen.

"It's going to be bloody cold."

"Swearing again, Mr Rudolf," said Steve.

"Oh shut up. And there won't be time to do much except bat on. We've only got four weeks left."

"Christ, another four weeks with you lot. I don't know how I'll survive," said Thomas.

"Well, you haven't got me to put up with much longer," said Simon.

"When are you leaving?" asked Win.

"Amritsar. That's two days' time."

"I don't know how we'll get on without you."

"Some more than others," said Thomas meaningfully. "I wonder who else will drop out." He looked about him.

"Like ten little Indians," said Conrad.

"I've dropped out already," said Rudolf. He poured himself some more whisky.

"Anyone else? Steve?" he asked. "Jen?" He hardly looked at Jen. Conrad pushed forward his glass.

"It's almost dead," said Rudolf.

"How are we going to bring in the New Year?" asked Simon.

"How's Rick?" asked Jen. Val looked up from her book.

"He's asleep. Craig's gone to see if he can get a doctor."

"Is it that serious?" Val shrugged.

"I think we ought to play charades," said Thomas. "Rudolf can do his impersonation of an upper-class twit."

"I beg your pardon."

"And Quintin will tell us the story of his life."

"Very boring I can assure you," said Quintin without looking up.

"What's for supper?" asked Steve.

"Simple roast duck and orange sauce," said Simon. "the *specialité du maison*."

"*De la maison*!" said Thomas.

"Oh sod off," said Simon. His brows knitted. Jen and Val whispered by the stove. Craig returned. A doctor followed him through the room.

"I wonder where they dug him up," said Rudolf. The others were silent.

"Well, here's to Rick," said Rudolf. "Let's hope it's half as bad as my dysentery." He poured himself another peg. "Preprandial nip. Marshall? Oops, sorry, there's none left."

"It's OK, I have some of my own." Marshall grinned. He flicked off the cap of his hip-flask and took a gulp.

"Would you care for some rum?" suggested Conrad. He fumbled in a duffle bag and drew out a bottle.

"We can have it in tea," said Thomas. "It's very good in tea. Boy!"

"I say, do you have to shout into my left ear?" protested Rudolf.

"I say, I'm afraid so old man. We're ordering a spot of tea, don't you know," said Thomas. "Boy! Tea for seven people." Steve whispered to Jen. They got up and went to the doorway.

"Aren't you having any tea?" challenged Thomas.

"We'll be back," said Steve. They passed the room where

Rick was being examined. They heard low voices. Steve kissed Jen on the ear. Jen turned and offered her mouth to be kissed.

"Poor Rick," she said.

"Poor Rick," mumbled Steve. He chewed Jen's lip. They staggered into the second bedroom. There were four beds in the room.

"It's so cold in here," said Jen.

"They don't light the stove till the evening."

"Let's get into bed."

"What, now?" Steve held Jen to stop her falling onto the bed.

"You won't leave me, will you Steve?"

"Why should I?" He smiled. Jen closed her eyes.

"Hold me. No, just hold me."

"I'm sorry," said Win as she slipped into the room. "I've come to change for dinner." Steve rolled over in bed.

"Hullo Win, what's the time? We must have fallen asleep."

"Six-thirty."

"I suppose we all ought to change," said Jen.

"You've heard about Rick have you?" Win continued.

"No?"

"He's got hepatitis. He'll have to fly home."

"Oh god! Poor old Rick. Is it very bad?"

"Infectious hepatitis, so the doctor said. It takes at least three months."

"But if it's infectious we'll all get it, won't we?"

"No, the doctor says it's not actually infectious. It's just called that. The germs are passed through water."

"I wonder how he got it."

. . .

Rick sat up in bed, cushioned by pillows. Steve stood at the foot of the bed.

"Happy New Year," said Steve.

"Happy New Year."

"Are you flying from Srinagar?"

"I think so. To Delhi, and then to London."

"What a way to go. You're dead lucky though. Think how cold it's going to be."

"I wouldn't mind."

"But you're ill, and that's that."

"Yup I've felt lousy for about a week now."

"Give my regards to England."

"Yes. Will you do one thing for me?"

"Anything you ask."

"Look after Val. She's a great girl."

"She don't need any looking after. But I will do all the same."

"Thanks."

"Ta-ra then."

"Goodbye." Steve returned to the sitting room. Kitbags stood by the armchairs. Marshall banged the standard lamp with his rucksack.

"We're moving out," said Thomas.

Two days later, when they had left Kashmir and were back on the Indian plain, Val rounded on Craig:

"You're pleased as hell, aren't you, that Rick got hepatitis. It's just what you hoped would happen so you could prove how bloody tough you are. Well, it doesn't impress me. He was beginning to undermine your authority, he was beginning to get you down, wasn't he. Don't deny it. I could see jealousy and disgust written all over your face.

"Perhaps you thought people were starting to listen to him more than they were to you. He was more patient than you are, Craig. He had a gentle nature. It sort of absorbed all the bitternesses that come out on a trip like this.

"But we're lumbered now, aren't we. The tyrant's back in control, there's no one to take our problems to now. We don't have any problems." Craig pressed his toe into the dust of the roadside.

"I'm sorry about Rick, Val. And I know you're upset that he's gone. You may even be right about me. I do find it easier to get on; people talk to me more. Even you talk to me more."

"How touching. Am I to believe that it makes any difference to you who you talk to or not? You're indifferent as hell to what people around you think. That's one thing I've learned about you. What's more I learned it the hard way."

"If you believe that then I suppose I've only myself to blame."

"Too right you have. You'd like to see us disappear one by one, like ten little Indians. So you can arrive back in London with an empty bus. You wanted Rudolf to leave."

"Didn't you?"

"Now Rick's gone. Simon's leaving. Who's next?"

"Simon always was leaving."

"You're fed up with us, aren't you. You'd like to push us all over a cliff if you could get away with it."

"I'm not fed up with you, Val."

"Oh, come on. I'm not going to buy that one. You think a bit of the old personal charm might stop the onslaught of criticism. Well I've had that, boyo. I'm going to show you what you really are. A tired old machine who's charmed too many and shagged the feeling out of himself."

"And there's no urge in you to reform this tired old specimen?"

"Not in the least. He can reform himself at the expense of no one's feelings but his own."

"Looks like I've met my match."

"That you have, my boyo." Val narrowed her eyes.

"In sheer aridity of soul, that is." Craig walked back to the Land Rover.

AMRITSAR, INDIA

Simon left at Amritsar. He checked into a hotel then walked about the town. For the first time in ten weeks he felt free. He felt sad as well but not enough to rock the positive calm of his freedom. It was as though he had jumped from a spinning roundabout of howling children into the tranquillity of the park and survived. It didn't matter that the park was Amritsar, hub of the Sikh religion. Simon, among the babble of cloth merchants, jewellers and swordsmiths, was at peace. His brow no longer knitted, no spasms crossed his face. He visited the Golden Temple, where a long arm of marble reached to the centre of a clear pool. Around the temple a tunnel of silks and carpets for sale represented the cloisters. Sikhs fat and thin bartered coolly; they twiddled their thumbs. For the first time in India Simon found salesmen who let him make his own choice. They waited to be approached. Simon felt that he understood these people better than he did the Hindu. He bought a religious sword. "And so to Bombay," he told himself.

LAHORE, PAKISTAN

THE SUN WAS COLDER than last time at the Park Luxury Hotel. Quintin sat in a deckchair on the lawn. In his hand were some plays by Sartre. Thomas stood near another deckchair. He hesitated to sit down. With thumbs in his trouser pockets he looked about. He watched Craig nearby under the Land Rover. Craig jacked up each wheel in turn to adjust the brakes.

Rudolf was still using a stick. He emerged from the darkness of the hotel. He saw Craig and lurched earnestly towards him.

"Do you want a hand?" he asked. Craig looked out from under the wheels.

"In exchange for a foot perhaps?" He smiled for a second. He played with his spanner and thought. "Yes. I'm adjusting the brakes," he said. "You can wield the jack if you like."

"Ah," said Rudolf. He took off his jacket and laid it on the bonnet of the Land Rover. He laid his stick there as well.

"You old fraud," said Craig.

"Now then," said Rudolf. He squatted on his haunches. Craig explained the workings of the jack.

"We'll get this done in no time," said Rudolf.

"There's plenty more to do," said Craig.

"Good Lord!" Thomas had not sat down. He was intrigued by the activities of Rudolf. "I never thought I'd live to see the day," he said. Quintin looked up. He saw Rudolf on his knees, his neck craned under the chassis. One hand pumped the handle of the jack. Rudolf's rump stuck in the air.

"Oh for an air-rifle," said Thomas.

"Greater love hath no man than this," mused Quintin.

"Talk about sucking up to Craig. It's ridiculous. All his lofty principles gone by the board."

"Occupational therapy."

"He must be in a pretty bad way then."

"We all are."

"Speak for yourself." Thomas stepped across the lawn. He stood over Rudolf. "So, it's come to this."

"If you knew what was good for you you'd be getting your hands dirty as well," taunted Rudolf.

"Rudolf has come to the conclusion," said Craig, "that standing around with one's hands in one's pockets is not a rewarding activity."

"I find it very rewarding," insisted Thomas. He rocked on his heels uncomfortably.

"I would have expected no more from our self-styled mandarin."

"I say, we've changed our tune a bit, haven't we, old Rudi-chops?"

"Look, clear off will you. You're being a pest. Craig and I have work to do."

"My goodness. Craig and I, eh? We *are* getting chummy. Workmates and all that."

"Bugger off Thomas," said Craig.

"Something tells me I'm not wanted. Well, work hard

chaps." Thomas removed himself with measured strides. He disappeared into the hotel. From the balcony on the first floor he looked down at the Land Rover. He leaned his elbow on the parapet. He propped his hand under his chin. Quintin, the Land Rover and the trailer formed a triangle. If he had been sitting on the other chair it would have been a trapezium. But he was not sitting in the chair. Circumstances had prevented him. Rudolf was working. That was why he was standing up here.

"If Rudolf had not wanted to work. If he had walked into town, then I would be sitting down there. I can picture myself in the deckchair. My life has been changed by Rudolf.

"But perhaps Rudolf could not avoid the decision to work. Perhaps it was written that on this third day of January Rudolf would change his tune. Who would have predicted it? I couldn't have." Thomas kicked his foot against the balustrade.

Win brought out an armful of washing. She laid it on the stone parapet to dry.

"This is our last chance," she said.

"My clothes will rot on me," said Thomas.

"I would have washed them if you'd asked."

"I don't believe in washing. I like to feel part of my clothes." Win laughed.

"You clothes certainly become part of you that way, and no mistake."

"It's only recently that people worried about smell."

"You're a strange boy, Thomas."

"I've inherited responsibilities of thought," said Thomas. "I see a long, continuous stream of thought through history, you see, attempting to discover things and reasons why we are here, what is meant by the dignity of human life and so on. Most people live without questioning it. They're so busy being happy or unhappy they don't have time to think. But a few of us are whittling away at the problem, trying to purify it and think of better reasons. The world is in a very slow process of growing up. But each generation of thinkers, if they make use of previous records, is a little bit wiser. I could be much wiser than Socrates, for example."

"And Bertrand Russell?"

"Potentially, yes. If I ever read more than he did, which is possible."

"But think of all the other experiences you'd miss if you did read everything."

"It's not so much *my* experience as collective experience," said Thomas. "You have to be conscious of what the rest of the world has gone through. Only then can you see all the permutations of what man can be."

"That sounds very philosophical; far too deep for me," said Win.

"You're one of the lucky people who aren't conscious of this terrible responsibility," said Thomas. "You're not worried by your national heritage, for example; what an Englishman stands for in relation to the rest of the world."

"I'm Welsh."

"Exactly," said Thomas. "Only England has accepted some responsibility for the state of the whole world."

"I'm sure that's wrong."

"Without imposing ideologies on it like Americanism or Communism."

"I don't believe an Englishman is better than anybody else," said Win.

"I do," said Thomas. He gripped the parapet. "He can be."

Win made her exit, whistling *Land of Hope and Glory*.

. . .

Quintin dined alone in the Salloos restaurant. It was late. The head waiter stood by the door to say goodnight to his clients. He was a fat, powerfully built man, but light on his feet. His moustache was fierce, his manner balanced. Quintin ate his steak with precision. The thick meat yielded graciously to his knife. Everything about the place was right. The cutlery opposite him was faultlessly laid, the lighting soft without gloom; music, if there had to be music, distant and nostalgic. An English couple three yards away spoke in cultivated voices. He had not yet used his napkin.

Quintin was not sad that the others had gone to a film without him. He wanted solitude to heal himself. He needed to build cushions of melancholy around him. The head waiter did him the honour of removing his plate.

"And for dessert, sir?"

"Fruit trifle, thank you." And oh for one more trifle, he thought. The last day in Kathmandu. The height of his brief ecstasy. It was better to be alone, he reflected. You were less vulnerable: you could close in your defences. "I'll come out of this one OK," he said. "Right as rain." A picture of Simon caught him unawares. He squeezed the rest of his bread roll into a lump. From the kitchen the head waiter brought a small tray. The tray was steady as his broad frame marched behind it. Quintin picked up his fork, and dropped it again. He gripped the edge of the table.

"I don't care what they think." He stared a long time at the neat place laid opposite him. His own fork had fallen, crooked. He picked it up and began to eat mechanically.

"Coffee, sir?"

"No thank you, just the bill." The empty bowl was removed. Quintin felt the humanity of the large waiter, the understanding which he extended to all his clientele. The waiter knew what was going on in the diner's head. Quintin shed a tear in the wish to be understood. "But what's his home like?" wondered Quintin. "Squawling kids, no sheets, the smell of cooking." They had no common ground except the subtle relationship between waiter and diner. "Beyond this room we are nothing."

"It's very embarrassing to love your neighbour," concluded Quintin, "or to be loved by him. We are better off alone." He left notes to cover the bill. He pushed his chair back with difficulty over the pile of the carpet. The English couple went on talking. Quintin walked soundlessly to the door. The head waiter didn't open it for him. His broad back filled the kitchen door.

"Where's bloody Marshall?" swore Thomas. The Land Rover waited outside the hotel. Craig blew into his clenched fist.

"He's gone to the American Consulate," said Conrad.

"Let's hope he's getting himself repatriated."

"He's fixing himself up with some shots."

"What does he need those for?"

"He really is a junky," said Steve.

"He's completing his file on Rudolf," said Quintin.

"Does gamma globulin mean anything to you?" wise-guyed Conrad.

"Aargh!" Steve clutched at his throat. "The dreaded gamma globules'"'

"Sounds like biological warfare."

"It is," said Conrad. "Marshall says it's an immunisation against hepatitis. We should all have a shot."

"It doesn't work," said Craig.

"He says it's eighty percent effective."

"Where does Marshall get it from anyway?"

"He has a friend at the consulate."

"It won't stop him getting hepatitis, if he's already got it."

"The doctor said it wasn't infectious anyway," said Win.

"Oo-er! I can feel the bugs crawling into my blood," said Val. A taxi drew up. Marshall transferred himself to the Land Rover.

"That's better. There's a fine shot of gamma globulin in that arm. Drive on, cabbie!"

BAMYAN, AFGHANISTAN

AFTER A DAY IN KABUL, they decided they had time to visit Bamyan, famous for its giant Buddha statues hewn into the side of a mountain. The figures seemed to rise directly out of the fruit and vegetable gardens on the flat alluvial plain.

"This must be the Buddhist equivalent of Mount Rushmore," said Marshall.

"I'm sure Mount Rushmore is much bigger and better," said Thomas.

"Why have we come here when it's off our route back home?" asked Jen, who was now counting the days.

"We could bash on and take the northern route via Mazar-i-Sharif," said Craig. "But that's a week we don't have." So they returned to Kabul and took the Russian road via Kandahar and Herat.

TEHRAN, IRAN

Marshall stood on the steps of the Central Post Office in Tehran. He held a telegram. With his other hand he suddenly threw a series of shadow punches.

"Sock it to 'em, baby!" Marshall ended with a Texan "Yee-haw!" then froze motionless.

"Yup. I have to go," he told Craig. He untied the tarpaulin and took his kitbag from the roof. He exhumed his brass plate from the bowels of the trailer and his two-man tent. He bequeathed a few books and pamphlets to his companions.

"Goodbye you suckers. It's gonna be damn cold where you're going." An orange taxi waited for him on the kerb. "Come to think of it, I won't be seeing any of you sons of bitches again in my whole life. So long." He settled into the cab and cried "Mush! Mush!" to the driver.

MIYANEH, IRAN

THERE WAS snow on the Elburz mountains outside Tehran. During the night it had rained, but in the morning the rain turned to snow. The road froze and crackled under the wheels. For a hundred miles flat highway skirted the mountains. After that a good surface wound through a shallow gorge. The snow stopped in the afternoon but the temperature fell. Condensation formed frost inside the cabin of the Land Rover. A thin sheet obscured the view outside. If ice was scraped away it soon formed again. Craig cleaned a small patch at the foot of the screen, and he hunched himself low to make use of it.

In darkness they came to Miyaneh. Lights shone from a tea-shed by the road. Large lorries were berthed nearby, with engines purring to keep warm.

Steve tore at the ropes on the roof-rack. The knots were like iron. After two minutes his hands were completely numb. Thomas tugged at another knot. His eyes watered; he found himself crying because of the cold.

The landlord gave the travellers a corner of the shed to sleep in. They drank chai with the lorry drivers. Soup steamed on charcoal. After three hours in the room the travellers felt their feet again.

"Whenever it gets really cold," said Craig, "I think of the Germans in 1941 on the Eastern Front, in their summer uniforms. That's what being cold is all about."

"It can't have been any worse than this," said Val.

"They were Germans anyway," said Thomas. "They deserved to die."

"Hear, hear," said Rudolf. "The same happened to Napoleon when he bit off more than he could chew."

"The common soldiers suffered while implementing the hare-brained schemes of their generals," put in Quintin.

"The thing is, will it get any colder? I think I could bear it if I knew it wouldn't get any colder," said Jen.

"It's as cold as I've ever known it," said Craig. Rudolf blew into his hands, although it was warm inside the room.

"Who's for a game of bridge?" suggested Thomas. But everyone was tired. They bedded down on the floor.

In the morning Val and Quintin made porridge. Steve prised open the icy tarpaulin and stacked the kitbags on the roof. Craig tried to start the engine.

"Fuck," he said. The oil was thick with cold. He could hardly turn the engine with the crank handle. Rudolf stood by with woollen mittens and a scarf; white clouds steamed from his mouth; water froze on the hairs in his nostrils.

"Can't we push her?" he suggested.

"Might do," said Craig. "We'd need the chains on." He took out a gas burner and played a flame over the manifold and the sump. "To heat up the oil," he said. Nearby, the Mack trucks were starting up. The drivers had been able to burn fires all night under their diesel engines. One driver drained oil from the sump and heated it indoors before pouring it back.

"Surely one of those could give us a tow," said Rudolf.

"They don't seem too interested." Craig continued to heat the engine block. "You could get out the chains." Rudolf looked about him.

"Where are the others? Lazy sods." He went to the trailer and took out a bag containing the chains. "How do they go?" he asked.

"Wait a minute," said Craig. He tried the starter again. He asked Rudolf to engage the starter while he turned the crank. But the moving parts seemed to be bound with glue. "Right. We'll put on the chains," said Craig. Seven faces watched from the window of the tea shed.

"Idle buggers," said Rudolf. He waved at them to come out. But they did not move.

"We need the jack now," said Craig. He jacked up a rear wheel and laid the chain underneath it. He lowered the jack and clipped the chains round the wheel. "They've got to be bloody tight," he said. He clipped on a tension spring.

"Does it matter which way round they go?" asked Rudolf, as he sorted the other chain.

"No." Craig walked to one of the big trucks. He returned to the Land Rover with a small Iranian. "This is Mustafa," said Craig. The Iranian laughed.

"Mustafa," he echoed.

"He's going to give us a tow." The truck backed onto the Land Rover and they fixed a hawser to the frame. The seven travellers came from the shed to watch the performance.

"Christ it's cold," said Thomas. He jumped up and down. Mustafa raised the revs of his lorry and slipped the clutch. The two vehicles swung into the road, and soon vapour came from the Land Rover's exhaust. Rudolf left the running board to release the hawser. Mustafa drove on.

"Fantastic things those trucks," said Steve. The passengers piled inside the frosted cabin. Snow clung to the floor. Thomas crawled into his sleeping bag. Jen spread a Nepalese blanket across three pairs of knees.

"It was so freezing this morning I didn't dare go to the loo," she said.

"You might have turned into a pillar of ice."

At midday they stopped at another tea shed. Small pots of stew bubbled on the stove. Conrad opened a tin of corned beef. He smashed the frozen contents on a tin plate.

"Sometimes the whole process of converting food into calories," said Quintin, "is so revolting that one would rather die." He toyed with the icy meat and flat bread.

"It all comes out the other end."

"You have to take the rough with the smooth," said Steve. He tipped his meat into a pot of soup.

"We're running out of peanut butter," said Thomas. "God, no wonder with Conrad about."

"My doctor says I have to eat peanut butter. I hate the stuff."

At nightfall they came close to the Turkish border. The cone of Mount Ararat gleamed in the moonlight. They stayed at another tea shed just inside Iran. Stray dogs roamed the frozen streets. Inside a long room the travellers sat on chairs against the wall. The tea was dispensed from a samovar. The villagers came to stare. They crowded into the road. Some drank tea, some could not afford to drink tea.

"Turkish types," said Craig. "Characteristic flat heads."

"Can't we get them to go away?" pleaded Jen.

"Ignore them."

"But we've got to sleep here."

"They'll clear off when we go to bed." Two paraffin lamps burned in the room. Steve and Conrad cooked on the stoves. The villagers laughed and jested among themselves.

"My god they look tough," said Thomas, "that one there looks really mean. Hullo Meanie, what are you staring at?

"You're lucky they can't understand you," said Rudolf, "otherwise our lives wouldn't be worth tuppence."

"They're just pretending to be tough – they have to be," said Quintin, returning an impudent stare. "I can imagine them descending in Mongol hordes and setting up their own barbarous empire. They don't look like a conquered race, do they?"

"We're in their country so we ought to respect them," said Jen.

"As far as I'm concerned they're foreigners," said Thomas. "Would you let your daughter marry one?"

"Yes!" said Jen. "If she wanted to."

"Well I think they're bloody marvellous," shouted Steve. "Imagine coming in and doing this in a fucking transport caff on the A1. They show hospitality such as you'd never find in the West."

"And in return they stare at you the whole evening," said Thomas.

"They think we're gods," said Conrad.

"Cobblers," said Steve. "They're waiting to see what they can nick off us in our sleep."

"One of us has to keep awake anyway," said Craig, "to run the engine every hour, otherwise it won't start tomorrow." They organised a rota, so that each person stayed awake for an hour, ran the engine for five minutes, then woke up the next person. At three o'clock Thomas woke Quintin.

"Is it cold out?" asked Quintin.

"Not as cold as last night."

"In other words bloody freezing." Quintin lay awake in his sleeping bag. Sometime in the next hour he would have to leave it and go into the cold. Until then his mind was busy, his fantasies trying to distract him from the task. When he first checked his watch it was twenty past three. He dreamed of the night at the Taj Mahal. Jerking his mind back he found it was five past four.

"Hell!" he whispered. Quintin shed his sleeping bag. The cold attacked his thighs. He pulled on two sweaters and stepped into his boots without lacing them. The ignition keys were on a chair.

The door squeaked. The stillness of the night rushed around him. He unlocked the driver's door and settled into the seat. The engine started first time. Quintin switched on the dashboard lights and watched the temperature gauge. As he revved the engine the needle crept towards the quarter mark. He listened to the engine. He heard the ringing of metal and the water in the cooling system, he heard the rhythm of the cylinders and the longer vibrations of the housing. When he switched off the engine, water gurgled in the system. Quintin stepped into the cold and locked the Land Rover door.

A blood-curdling yell exploded by his neck. He swung round. It was the howl of a savage beast. His terror produced a yell in return. Quintin howled like a dog at the dog's howl. "You bastard!" he cursed. His bootlaces clicked as they gained the squeaking door. "Lord preserve us."

"What was that?"

"Only a dog. Scared the shit out of me." It was Steve's turn to keep the vigil.

IRAN-TURKISH BORDER

AFTER BREAKFAST they drove to the border, a broad pass under the shadow of Ararat. It took two hours to get through the border. The Iranians and Turks did not like to be rushed. They inspected the luggage, counted cameras, entered passport particulars, and stamped the customs carnet, with suspicion.

"No hashish?"

"Yok!"

Ten miles from the border lay Dogubayazit with a modern hotel. They stopped for an early lunch.

"Turkish food!"

"Decent bread!" In the large dining room Thomas and Conrad ordered a variety of dishes, meat and beans, spinach with fried egg, rice, stuffed tomato. They soaked up the gravy with chunks of rustic bread. The others were more moderate.

"Christ! I'd forgotten what real bread was like," mumbled Thomas. Tea and yoghurt followed.

At one o'clock Craig returned to the Land Rover.

"We want to get to Erzurum tonight," he said. At ten past one the Land Rover moved off. Until Eleskirt the journey was flat and uneventful. Snow fell lightly. They passed a lorry which had stopped; the driver was putting on chains. Two more lorries lay at the side of the road. Craig stopped.

Rudolf left the warmth of the cabin to help him put on the chains. Thomas got out to lend a hand. When they entered the Land Rover again the others were singing.

"Extremes like this make men most unnatural," said Quintin.

"Speak for yourself."

The road wound in a great circle up the mountainside. Daylight was already being sucked from the land. Craig saw red tail-lights ahead of him. At a hair-pin bend an articulated lorry had left the road. The bulk of its cargo lay at a steep angle in the ditch. A Ford Transit was out of action farther up. Two hundred yards beyond that was a queue of traffic.

"We are waiting for a snow-plough," said a German driver. In front of the Land Rover a pair of Mercedes lorries waited: Militzer & Münch Internationale Spedition GmbH.

"We'll stick behind these," said Craig. "They know their job." The snow fell thicker as they waited. In the half-light, drifting flakes obscured the road.

The snow-plough came, an orange Galion. Four huge wheels clad with chains below the driver's cabin, a broad scraper under its belly and guiding wheels in front at the end of a long trunk. A bus without chains had slid into the ditch. The snow-plough tossed out a hawser. With its four powered wheels shooting out snow it pulled the bus along the ditch, and out.

The column moved forward. Militzer & Münch crept to the top of the pass. Snow-plough sheds glowed behind an open fire.

"Can't we warm up there?" asked Jen.

"We've got to get on," said Thomas. But the traffic halted. No lorries were coming the other way. Craig kept the engine running to work the heater: but he glanced at the fuel gauge. If they were to be stuck here all night they had only half a tank left.

"Who's for a game of bridge?" asked Thomas. He switched on the interior light. Thomas, Quintin, Rudolf and Val played bridge. From the top of the pass they saw the lights of lorries like luminous feelers of beetles, testing their way down the narrow descent. The snow-plough worked in a blaze of headlights. The queue edged forward, and stopped. The Land Rover wheels locked on the ice and the vehicle slid forward a few yards to nudge Militzer & Münch on the bumper.

"Nice of them to be there," said Rudolf. "Two spades." After Rudolf had won the game the traffic moved. But it was three hours before they reached Horasan at the foot of the pass: seven o'clock. They stopped for tea. Twenty people crowded round the central stove of the tea-house.

"We can sleep here if you want," said Craig, "or we can get to Erzurum in two hours for a hotel."

"Not another night on the floor," said Rudolf.

"Being stared at by all and sundry," said Thomas.

They stayed in the Kristal Palas at Erzurum, four to a room, no bed-linen, no hot water and a single tin stove for each jumbled storey. The proprietor was fat and amorous. He embraced Craig as an old friend.

"He must be getting a rake-off," said Thomas.

"What? On two-and-six a night?" Tea was served to everyone. Half-dressed Muslims wandered into the rooms. There was a sound of spitting in the washing alcoves. A radio resonated from the ground floor where card games were in progress.

"We'll go across the street for some food," said Craig. They entered a restaurant with white tablecloths. They ordered wine, salads and kebab. After the dessert they filled themselves with bread and wine.

"Well, this is a kind of respite," said Craig. "We have worse to come again."

CENTRAL TURKEY

THOMAS WROTE IN HIS DIARY:

Tearing ourselves from the lecherous hugs of the hotelier we said goodbye to snow-clad Erzurum. The road is not too mountainous until near Erzincan. We had lunch at the top of a pass, by the snow-plough sheds. I saw what I think were wolf-tracks. But the road was clear, the weather calm. We were expecting more delays, however. To avoid the mountains we took a cross-country route on dirt roads, winding through gorges, competing with the railway, surprised to find that among these ridges behind the Black Sea mountains, the winter is milder.

The cold brings us together. This is our last pioneering effort before getting back to civilisation. People are beginning to wonder what will happen to us after the trip. Will they see each other again? Who will write to whom? What, for instance, will happen to the S/J liaison? Will Rudolf make another bid for holy matrimony? V seems to remain faithful to R. Interesting sociological phenomena, but how relevant to the after-life? Bollocks.

Craig's promise of foul weather was completely discredited.

We sail into an early spring. After a night at a one-horse hotel in Reşadiye we come to fields without snow where sods are fresh turned by the plough, larks tweedle out of sight, and the grass blushes new green into its cheeks. We could be on the Sussex Downs in April.

Steve ran his hands along the lines of a boat beached on the lakeside.

"It's like Noah's Ark," he said. Jen let her hand slide over the curved wood.

"Steve?"

"What?" He did not look at her. He walked to the prow of the boat.

"Never mind." Jen followed him to the prow. She looked at the lakeside. Green reeds extended through the water. "Isn't this lovely," she said.

"Fair enough," said Steve.

"It's lovely because it's spring," she went on. "And it's part of you." Steve laughed.

"I'm nothing to do with spring."

"Yes you are, you change with the seasons. At the moment you're strong and keen and bursting with new life. I like to watch you stride about, then stop and look at things. I feel part of me is looking as well."

"That's a mite fanciful isn't it?"

"Steve?" He looked at her.

"You're always asking me questions."

"No I'm not."

"With your eyes. Great asking eyes. They're like saucers." She looked down.

"I don't mean to ask you questions, Steve."

"Stop following me around then."

"That's a very cruel thing to say, to someone who's supposed to be -."

"What?"

"You've changed, that's all."

"Like you said, I change with the seasons."

"I wish it was winter again." Steve laughed. "I wish it was so cold that we had to fight each other to keep warm."

"I'd lay you flat any day of the week."

"Would you?" Jen clutched at Steve's arm. He shook her off.

"Leave me alone, Jen."

"What have I done wrong?"

"Nothing. You're a very sweet lass. Leave me alone."

"I can't. Unless you tell me why."

"'Why – why - why'. There you are – questions."

"I'm sorry." Steve did not walk away. He looked at the mountains on the other side of the lake. "I can't help being in love with you, Steve. Are you bored with me?" Steve turned. He squeezed Jen's hands.

"No, Jen, no." Jen pressed her forehead against his arm. She sighed.

"Yes you are." The Land Rover horn sounded.

"Come on, it's dinner time," said Steve. "I'll race you back!" But they didn't run. They walked under apple-blossom without a word.

ISTANBUL, TURKEY

VAL DESCENDED the stairs of the hotel. The Turk behind the reception desk gave her a half-smile. She descended the steps of the hotel entrance. It was dark outside. Yellow lamps in the street lit the cobbles and picked out the bonnet of the Land Rover. Craig leaned over the front seat. He was removing items from the safe under the seat. He heard Val's voice behind him.

"Hullo," it said.

"Hullo." He continued with his work. He stood up and sensed Val behind him. He smelled her scent and the wax of the lipstick which she had put on.

"What are you doing?" she asked.

"I'm taking the Land Rover to be serviced." Val did not move. "I thought you were going out with the others." Val remained motionless, although her scent suffused the air.

"Can I come with you?"

"What do you know about servicing Land Rovers?"

"I want to come with you."

"Oh." Craig sat in the driving seat. He unlocked the passenger door. Val slid onto the front bench. It took twenty minutes to drive to the garage. They didn't exchange a word.

The servicing bays were brightly lit. Craig centred the Land Rover above the hydraulic lift.

"What do we do now?" asked Val.

"We get out," said Craig. He helped Val to jump down as the car rose. "Unless you want to get wet."

"Help!" Val smiled at Craig. He held a folder of documents under his arm.

"Washing, greasing, oil-change, oil-filter, everything very good," said Craig in Turkish-English. "We've slapped on the old make-up tonight then, haven't we."

"Don't you like it?"

"We'll get something to eat," said Craig. He strode down a street past cheap hotels with wooden signboards. Val skipped beside him.

"I haven't got any money," she said.

"You can pay me back."

"Where are you going?" Val was panting.

"Little place I know. Very cheap."

"Will I get jumped on?"

"Don't you want a bit of excitement?"

"Yes." Val stared at him as they strode along.

They came to a square crowded with taxis and lorries. At one end the city wall of Theodosius towered above it. Around the square, houses were stacked like wooden boxes. Interiors glowed behind blue-framed windows. Bare-tabled rooms led to smoky kitchens. There were ten or so primitive restaurants in the square.

"First we buy a bottle of wine," said Craig. He entered a shop. The shelves were laden with tins, bottles, boxes and balls of string, all faded. Craig grabbed a bottle and swept dust from the neck. The shopkeeper opened it.

"This very good." They crossed the square. Turks greeted them with friendly jeers. Craig descended steps into a cellar room. The chef sprang up to shake his hand, and ushered them to a table. It was covered with oil-cloth. Other diners, with moustaches and caps, cupped glasses of raki in their heavy hands and drank.

Craig and Val entered the kitchen to choose their dishes. They returned to the table. Craig poured the wine.

"Tonight I'm seeing you as you really are," said Val. "This is what you would do on your own."

"No-one should drink a bottle of wine on his own."

"But you would have brought it here and made friends with the natives."

"I used to do that. But I'm tired of making endless shows of bonhomie."

"Don't you like these people?"

"There's a difference between appreciating local colour, and actually getting to grips with people and all their hopes and fears; their tragedies."

"I thought you were the self-styled brother of the Asian working class; they seem to greet you like a long-lost brother."

"No. It's a charade. We're not like them and they're not like us. I couldn't live like them, however much I empathise with them.

"You don't have to. You can be like Lawrence of Arabia: an Arab one minute, and hob-nobbing with Bernard Shaw and the Archbishop of Canterbury the next."

"I don't have friends in high places."

"Well, you do have friends," she said, laying her hand on his.

"A few." Craig felt the texture of her palm, which he had forgotten. After dinner they fetched the Land Rover. It was wet and shining. "I want to show you something," he said. He drove through the breach in the city wall, descending to the sea. On the coastal road he stopped the car. They got out and walked along a breakwater. Water slapped against the hulls of boats in the marina. Across the Sea of Marmara lay the lights of Asia, a tall block of army barracks, mosques, Hydarpasa rail ferry terminal. The headlights of ferries plied towards the narrow Bosphorus.

"What did you want to show me?" asked Val, looking about her.

"This," said Craig.

"Silly," said Val. She hugged herself against his shoulder. "I think it's lovely." They sat on the sea wall, dangling their legs over the concrete.

"What are you running away from?" asked Val.

"Stagnation, attitudes, what do you mean anyway?"

"You always seem to want change. And if you can't get it you sulk like a little boy. You've been sulking for three months."

"I've been bored, if that's what you mean."

"You need to settle down. You want children and a nagging wife."

"Do I?"

"Whatever you want, it's not this."

"What?"

"Being the head of a ridiculous conga-dance through Asia." Craig was silent. Val continued: "We people mean nothing to you. You despise us."

"No, but I find it hard not despise myself."

"Your single triumph is to get away from us. Or to take one of us aside, like me, and plunder us. And when we get back to London we are filed away in a cabinet as expedition number so-and-so, three women, nine men, one proposal, one case of hepatitis, fourteen bangs."

"I'm not protesting; but it's not like that at all."

"It may not have been. But that's what it's become. You're too old. You've been at this too long." Craig got up.

"Let's go," he said.

. . .

Rudolf folded his airmail copy of *The Times*.

"Ah!" he said. He rose from his armchair in the hotel foyer and strode towards Craig. Val tugged Craig's arm.

"Come on," she said.

"Ah what?" asked Craig.

"Final briefing," said Rudolf. "I'm leaving tomorrow by plane."

"So you're not seeing it through to London?"

"Frankly, between me and you, I've seen enough of Europe. And I've had my fill of travelling for a while. My guts are behaving like a sieve," Rudolf giggled. "Don't worry about me. I'll find my own way back."

"Who's going to help me put the chains on?"

"Haha. You haven't got them trained, have you."

"Come on," said Val.

"Haha," said Rudolf. He waved his paper. "I'll say goodbye to you tomorrow."

"D'you think he'll ask Jen again?" wondered Val.

"No. Jen has problems of her own."

"Poor Jen." Craig closed the door of his room and they faced each other like sparring beasts.

CARINTHIA, AUSTRIA

SNOW SWEPT over the Alps

"It's not as bad as bloody Turkey, is it," said Thomas. The windscreen wipers took away each invasion of snow. But every time a new horde of flakes returned. Corpses of snowflakes piled up at the foot of the windshield. The headlights picked out the wheeling armies before they smacked against the bonnet. Craig drove slowly.

"We should have stopped in Bad Aussee," said Jen. "You knew it was going to be like this." No one responded. "Now we won't get to Salzburg till about ten."

"Never mind, lass," said Steve.

"I do mind," Jen persisted. "I'm fed up with being cooped up in this Land Rover. I wanted a bath, and an early night. We all need one."

"We're all as tired as you are," said Thomas. "It doesn't help to moan about it."

"I'm not moaning. I think we should stop."

"Unlucky," said Conrad. Steve began to sing *On Ilkley Moor Baht 'at*. Thomas joined in Jen sighed "Oh!" and laid her head and forearm against the front seat. Thomas suddenly recited with his arms folded:

"And so it was that, while they were in this bloody Land Rover, the days were accomplished that she should be delivered."

"What are you saying, Thomas?" asked Jen.

"Isn't it obvious? You're pregnant."

"You know!" screamed Jen. Steve took her arm.

"Come on Jen. There's no need to get all worked up again."

"You told him I'm pregnant."

"Hushhh!" cautioned Steve. "Let's not have a scene. Take it out on me, not the others."

"You promised not to tell anyone."

"I didn't tell him. He must have guessed."

"I guessed," said Thomas. Steve stroked Jen's arm.

"Please, pull yourself together. It's only a few days to go now"

"And then what? What am I supposed to do after that? Run to Daddy and ask him to forgive me?"

"We'll think of something."

"But you're going away. Up North. I won't see you again."

"That's not true. You've just got to trust me, that's all. Now Jen, get yourself some sleep on my shoulder."

"Steve!" She hammered her fists against his shoulder. "How can you be so calm? You're as much to blame as I am. You should be taking responsibility."

"And you should have taken your bloody pills!" Steve shouted, finally.

CALAIS, FRANCE

Squeezed between trucks in the hold of the Channel ferry, enveloped in diesel fumes, the Land Rover and trailer suddenly looked small again. It had carried them all that way through snow and desert, crowded cities and desolate mountains. Now it was within sight of home, and probably - unless it was hastily serviced and sent out again - destined for the scrapheap.

Craig stretched out on a bench in the main passenger lounge and tried to sleep. Jen had calmed down a little after her outburst. She and Steve sniffed perfumes in the duty-free shop.

"I love Chanel No 5," she said.

"Anyone would at that price," said Steve. But later, while she was drinking coffee, he sneaked back and bought a bottle.

On their way out of Dover they stopped at a fish-and-chip shop and gorged themselves on battered cod and chips soaked in vinegar.

"We've arrived!" said Thomas. "For three-and-a-half months I've been looking forward to this treat."

"You could've just stayed here and pigged yourself," said Steve.

Craig drove in silence from Dover. Without much further

conversation they crawled through the London suburbs and finally reached King's Cross Station.

"This is it, folks," said Craig. No-one had prepared a farewell speech. Six of them unloaded their belongings from the Land Rover and hung about as if wondering what happened next. Steve and Jen decided to look for coffee. Thomas was heading for Watford, Quintin for Kensington, Win for Wales and Conrad for Heathrow Airport. Val hovered.

"Am I coming with you?" she asked Craig.

"Please yourself. I'm heading for Battersea."

NOTES

ABOUT THE AUTHOR

David Shirreff is a writer of plays, musicals, fiction and non-fiction. He has travelled widely as a journalist for various publications including *The Economist* and *The Wall Street Journal*. Besides *Overland 1970* there are several other works of fiction and biography in the pipeline including *Angels Over Lusatia*, a trilogy set in the mining region of eastern Germany. The first volume is a biography of the German rock-poet Gerhard Gundermann.

Other books by David Shirreff:

Dealing with Financial Risk, Profile Books, 2004

Don't Start From Here: We Need a Banking Revolution, Crunch Books, 2014

Vulkan: the evil empire's last gamble, Crunch Books, 2015

Break Up The Banks! A Practical Guide to Stopping the Next Global Financial Meltdown, Melville House, 2016

Check for the latest titles at www.crunchbooks.org

www.ingramcontent.com/pod-product-compliance
Lightning Source LLC
Chambersburg PA
CBHW071450040426
42444CB00008B/1279